The Trouble with Old Lovers

A play

Angela Huth

Samuel French — London
New York - Toronto - Hollywood

Please see page iv for further copyright information

Printed at Redwood Books, Trowbridge, Wiltshire.

THE TROUBLE WITH OLD LOVERS

First presented by the Haymarket Theatre, Basingstoke, on 9th February, 1995, in association with WM Franklyn TYL, with the following cast:

Alice	Joanna Van Gyseghem
Tom	William Franklyn
Edward	John Quayle
Laura	Frances White
Mary	Tracey Childs

Directed by Robert Chetwyn
Designed by Elroy Ashmore
Lighting by David Ripley

CHARACTERS

Alice, early 50s
Tom, mid to late 50s
Edward, early 50s
Laura, late 40s
Mary, late 30s-early 40s

The action takes place in Tom's and Alice's house, somewhere in the West Country

ACT I

Time—the present

ACT I

SCENE 1

Tom's and Alice's house somewhere in the West Country. Late afternoon in early Autumn

A kitchen, which is more like a sitting-room, in a country house: evidence that much of Tom's and Alice's life takes place therein. The functional end of the room is the L part, just out of sight: the living end, with a large table, old dresser and ailing sofa, is the part we see. French windows, upstage, lead to the makings of a terrace and a vague garden beyond. The table, downstage, is covered with papers, letters, gardeners' catalogues, a pot and five mugs of tea, the remains of lunch for one, and two seed trays planted with small green shoots

Tom sits at the table, pencil in hand, concentrating on a catalogue, making notes. He listens to music on a record player. He takes sips from various mugs of tea, each one unsatisfactory, but has the air of a man who is enjoying himself. Off stage a door bangs. Tom shifts, surprised. He looks at his watch, hastily switches off the record player and sweeps a bit of earth from the table to the floor and hides his lunch plate under a pile of catalogues

Alice enters, carrying an umbrella. She is wearing the kind of silk suit that is kept by people of her age for going to weddings, and a very out-of-date feather hat. She looks at her husband and the muddle all about him, for a long time

Tom does not break his study of the catalogues or look up at her. Eventually Alice undoes the top button of her jacket. She just might be very slightly drunk. Tom puts down his pencil, raises his head

Tom Alice! Your feathers are all ruffled!

Alice The weather changed. The skies opened and drenched the youngish couple.

Tom Enjoyed yourself, though, did you?

Alice Good champagne. You should have come.

Tom I'd no desire to watch dear Elizabeth walk down the aisle to so precarious a future.

Alice Patrick's all right.
Tom Not for Elizabeth.
Alice Dare say you're the best judge of that. Oh, you didn't manage to take
out the pie, then?

*Alice comes up the table, rustles through the papers and finds the lunch plate.
She examines a half-eaten sandwich*

Tom No time. Choosing things for the terrace.
Alice It would have been quicker, actually, than making a disgusting fish
paste sandwich. (*She puts the plate down with distaste*) Hope you've been
very careful in your choice. You can judge a man by his garden furniture,
you know.

*Alice undoes the rest of her jacket. Tom goes back to his catalogues, takes no
notice. Alice flings the jacket off. She stands there, fingering the lace of a
beautiful satin petticoat. Hard to tell whether her slight randiness is a tease,
or real. Tom doesn't notice either way. Alice sighs. She picks up his huge old
jersey from a chair*

Do you mind? (*She clears enough space on the table to perch herself close
to Tom. Clumsily, she leaps on to the table and positions herself in another
faintly provocative pose*) I can't remember. Did you ever sleep with Carol
Barkshot? The Carol Barkshot who wore fox furs? (*She flings his jersey
round her neck as if it was a fur*)
Tom Why? Was she there?
Alice She was. Still in furs.
Tom (*vague*) I think I may have hopped into bed with her once or twice.

*Long silence. Alice looks down on Tom, ticking things on a list, with a small
smile*

Alice Isn't it odd how Englishmen never go to bed, except on their own? As
soon as it's with someone else — have you noticed? They tell you they've
hopped, jumped, or even popped into bed, whatever that might mean ...
Tom Mind out. You're sitting on the thing I want. (*He plucks a catalogue
from under her*) Victorian cast-iron seats. What d'you think?
Alice (*struggling into the jersey*) Poor old Carol Barkshot.
Tom What? (*Pause*) Why poor old Carol Barkshot?
Alice Well, I mean. Imagine it from her point of view. There she is, sitting
up in bed, nothing on but her furs, waiting. She looks across the room to
this naked man, this lover who had such potential in his pinstripe suit —
this lover who she thought moved quite normally in his clothes, and there

he is suddenly hopping towards her like a demented kangaroo. (*Pause*) I wouldn't have thought it was a tremendously good start, myself.

Alice slides off the table, pulls down the jersey. It comes down to her knees. Tom can now look at her

Tom Speak to her?
Alice Who?
Tom Carol?
Alice Oh, Carol Barkshot. No, of course I didn't speak to Carol Barkshot. I don't know her, do I? Except by reputation.
Tom Tea? How many upright chairs would you say we need? Seventy-nine pounds each.

Long pause while Alice tries to think

Alice Four.
Tom Just what I thought. Three hundred and sixteen pounds. That's it, then. Mission completed.

Tom gets up, holding the teapot. He goes off to the kettle

Alice, not quite knowing what to do with herself, moves to the sofa. She settles into a comfortable position

Alice You'll be wanting to know how Elizabeth looked.
Tom (*off*) Not really.
Alice Well, not at all bad. Honestly. Considering. In fact, quite good.
Tom (*off*) Good.

Tom returns with the teapot. He looks into all the mugs on the table, then goes to the dresser to get two clean ones

Alice She was subtle enough to wear magnolia ——
Tom She was quite rich in subtleties, Elizabeth. (*He pours tea for them both*)
Alice Well, I suppose it might have been taken for white from a distance. But I was quite close to her. I saw it was definitely magnolia. (*She takes the tea*) Did you do the potatoes?
Tom By God, I didn't. I'm sorry. Meant to. Takes an extraordinary long time, garden furniture, getting it right.
Alice She had a very, very long train. To counteract her height, I suppose.
Tom Look, I'm not terribly interested in Elizabeth's wedding dress ——

Alice Thousands of seed pearls, hand sewn. Can't be much unemployment in the wedding dress business, I don't imagine. She had three enormous bridesmaids. Vast galleons, they were. Compared with them, of course, Elizabeth was absolutely ... Sorry. I'm boring you with my eye for detail. (*She sighs*) Tell me what you've been ordering.

Tom (*pleased*) I've gone a bit mad, I think. "Barrister goes over top".

Alice You haven't!

Tom I have! Right over the top. One of those vast sunshades for the table, four wrought-iron armchairs, two urns from Chatsworth ——

Alice Wonderful.

Tom Might as well take advantage of living in this mail-order age.

Alice Absolutely. (*She holds up her mug for more tea*) There's just a possibility I may have drunk more than I'd planned.

She looks up at Tom who stands rock still

You're going round and round.

Tom Try shutting your eyes.

Alice does so

I almost decided on one of those ultra modern no-fuss barbecues. A hundred and forty-nine pounds, special offer. But I just managed to resist.

Alice I think you should carry on. Resisting, I mean. (*She opens her eyes*) It's worse with them shut.

Tom I was thinking, though, once the terrace was finished ... we might even start to entertain a little. Only this afternoon I was thinking to myself: we don't see many people, do we?

Alice No, thank God.

Tom It might be rather nice. Occasionally.

Alice (*smiling to herself*) So it might.

Tom You know, nothing very elaborate. Just a few friends round. Marinated chops. Herb sausages. *Fraises du bois* plucked from the edge of the terrace itself ...

Alice And then, just as we'd got it all out there, down comes the rain.

Tom You're so practical, Alice.

Alice puts a hand out to him. He helps her up off the sofa

Tom Improving?

Alice I'm all right.

Alice's arms flail slightly. Tom quickly pulls a wooden chair away from the table. Grateful, Alice holds on to the back of it

I had a funny time at the reception. I didn't talk to anyone much. I found myself standing on a chair ——

Tom Standing on a chair?

Alice Don't worry, no-one noticed. Standing on a chair looking down at them all. Thinking.

Tom You do the oddest things when I'm not there.

Alice Do you know what I was thinking? (*She becomes glazed by her reverie*) I was thinking I would have liked to have taken a long golden thread and woven it between all the people there who had at some time been involved with each other. Oh! The intricacies of the pattern. You can't imagine. Almost all the guests would have been caught up in a vast cobweb. I found myself laughing. Someone said, "What's the matter, Alice? Why are you laughing?"

Tom You must have looked fairly dotty standing on a chair at a wedding reception, laughing to yourself.

Alice I couldn't have explained about the cobweb. They wouldn't have understood. So I accepted help down from the chair.

Tom Good.

Alice But I couldn't get rid of the picture in my mind. The more I moved about the more I saw its threads weaving in and out, joining the most unlikely people. I thought: if only they could all see what I can see. A lot of them, husbands and wives, might be quite surprised.

Tom Yes, well. In a small society — inevitable.

Alice (*after a long pause*) And then Edward Harrison came up to me ——

Tom Struggling through the cobweb ——

Alice Remember him?

Tom I do remember Edward Harrison. Yes. (*Long pause*) You know, in summer, I can sit out on the terrace reading my briefs. Once the sunshade is all set up.

Alice So you can.

Tom I shall like that.

Alice But you know you're never any good at working at home.

Tom It'll be different, on the terrace. Was he with his wife?

Alice Laura was there, yes.

Tom Talk to her?

Alice A word or two. (*Pause*) Did Laura always have that trouble with her teeth?

Tom What trouble with her teeth?

Alice Well, you know. You must have noticed. When she smiles you can see her middle teeth aren't quite in the middle. She's one of those people whose middle teeth are definitely to one side.

Tom Really. Can't say I ever noticed. She had a pretty smile, far as I remember, and lovely feet.

Alice Oh, her feet. They're still fine. (*No longer dizzy, she begins to pace about, vaguely tidying up*) God knows, poor girl, her mother should have done something about them. Had them swung round when she was a child. It's so mean, mothers who ignore their children's peculiar teeth. (*Fast*) Think of all those people with teeth that cross over, teeth that protrude, teeth so large the lips can never quite shut. None of them need have suffered if only their stupid mothers had bothered. Poor Laura.

Tom I don't think Laura suffered, much.

Alice Well, I hope she didn't. (*Pause*) But how do you know? Was teeth one of your conversations? I would have thought a gentleman shouldn't talk about teeth to a lady whose teeth are a problem.

Tom Al-ice. Do stop.

Alice I'm amazed you never noticed, that's all.

Tom Anyway, what *is* Edward now?

Alice He's still in wine, he said. Very high up in wine, now, as a matter of fact.

Tom Excellent place to be high up in.

Alice Funnily enough, he asked just the same question about you. "What is Tom now?" he asked. "Still a barrister?" "What do you think?" I said. "Does Tom look like one of those flibberty-gibbets who keeps switching professions? Of course he's still a barrister," I said. "One day he'll be a judge."

Tom I won't, you know.

Alice Well, that's what I told Edward.

Tom Nice of you. Shall I do the potatoes now?

Alice That would be very kind.

Tom (*making no move, but looking at her*) Had you forgotten your hat?

Alice has plainly forgotten it. She laughs, takes it off and strokes it

Alice Poor feathers. I bought it when I was a student in Paris.

Tom So you tell me at every wedding and every funeral.

Alice We all wore them. They were the rage.

Tom (*still not moving*) Shall we have baked? Less trouble.

Alice Fine. I've got to do an essay by Wednesday.

Alice goes to the dresser, puts her hat on a jar, then feels down the cushions of the sofa. She comes up with a pair of round, gold-rimmed glasses. She puts them on and turns to Tom

Do you suppose all over England middle-aged husbands are about to do the potatoes while their middle-aged wives are about to wrestle with *The Ancient Mariner*?

Tom It's the way things seem to be going. No more jokes now with women. No more relaxing chit-chat, at the end of a long day, about the children. Can't go out to dinner these days without being got at by a grey-haired late starter in the over-populated field of adult education. You've scarcely picked up your soup spoon before some wrinkled old student batters you with an earnest question about whether feminism was the driving force in the heart of Fanny Price.

Alice (*hopelessly trying to assemble an untidy pile of books beside her, laughing*) Perhaps you should give some serious thought to such things.

Tom Fanny Price a feminist? Who *are* the teachers these days?

Alice I'm sorry it all annoys you so much. But it's worth it. Think — just another five and a half years and I'll have my degree.

Tom (*amazed*) I hadn't realized you had that much longer to go. It seems to have been going on for ...

Alice It's not long to wait for letters after your name.

Tom (*quietly*) Five and a half more years of no time to take my suit to the cleaners, no time to ring the plumber, no time to ... The continuing case of Samuel Coleridge Taylor versus my supper. Samuel Coleridge Taylor nearly always winning.

Alice Darling, I'm sorry. I keep saying I'm sorry. (*She sits on the sofa*)

Tom Oh, I only mind from time to time. I mean, you put up with my terrace, I put up with your Swinburne. Swinburne and Terrace. Rather a good name for a company, don't you think? My wife and I run a little company called Swinburne and Terrace ——

Alice Please, Tom. I've got to concentrate. (*She opens various books*)

Silence. Tom gazes upon his studious wife. She has no notion of his contained restlessness

Tom Sorry! In the old days we used to play Scrabble. I taught you lots of new words.

Alice (*not looking up*) Farad, cully, zymo. So very useful.

Tom (*apologetic, indicating her book*) Is it, in fact, Swinburne tonight?

Alice Byron.

Tom Ah. (*He listens to the silence. Tentatively*) Don Juan? Likely to be a long session.

Alice (*trying for patience*) Tom! I've got to get through the whole first canto before I go to bed.

Tom Sorry, sorry, sorry. Didn't mean to interrupt. I was merely trying to work out if I should get going on the *entire* supper, or just the potatoes?

Alice If you're trying to make me feel guilty ——

Tom I'm not trying to make you feel guilty ——

Alice Well, if you are, you're not succeeding. Leave the whole thing to me. It's just that damned wedding has put out my schedule.

She pushes the books away. Some fall on the floor. Tom leaps to pick them up

No, leave them. I'm no longer in the mood.

Tom Thank God for that. I mean, you should give yourself a break sometimes. Saturday evenings. You push yourself too hard. All work and no ... at your age.

Alice Thanks.

Tom In the good old days, once a mother was shot of her children she'd take her chance to relax. See more of her friends, take up gardening ... I don't know. All the things she'd been meaning to do for years. Pottering about with her little trug, secateurs in hand.

Alice And die of a withered brain. Very funny. I haven't been longing to do a lot of mindless things all those years, you know perfectly well. Quite the opposite. The more I saw of the children labouring through their exams, the more I longed to make up for my own lost education and catch up with them at last. Will I ever catch up with them? I sometimes wonder. And why should I want to? But please don't let's have another discussion about all this. It's one of our more fruitless arguments.

Tom Quite.

Alice I wouldn't mind a drink. I know it's early.

Tom Do you think ...?

Alice I'm perfectly all right now. Sober as a barrister.

Tom goes to the dresser, pours two drinks, passes one to Alice

Alice (*after a pause*) You know your idea about a little entertaining?

Tom What about it? I wasn't being very serious.

Alice Oh, I'd hoped you were. Because I've a surprise for you. We're starting tomorrow.

Tom What?

Alice Two very old friends are coming.

Tom (*horrified*) What? We never have people on a Sunday.

Alice Well, sorry, but they're coming.

Tom Who? Sunday's always been our day. At least, it used to be till Byron and Co. took over.

Alice I got in a muddle. At the wedding ——

Tom I should say you did. Standing on a chair ——

Alice They asked themselves, really. (*Pause while she takes another drink*) Thanks, Laura and Edward.

Tom (*quietly*) But that's not possible.

Alice They're definitely coming.

Tom I mean: Laura loathes the country.

Alice So does Edward.

Tom Well, then. You'll have to put them off.

Alice How can I put them off? I've no idea where they're staying. I didn't ask Edward who their host was. It didn't seem to matter.

Tom We could get on to the police. Get them to put our message on the radio.

Alice They only do that in an emergency.

Tom This *is* an emergency! (*Dejected*) The thought of such a visit completely spoils my evening.

Alice I thought it was already spoilt by my Byron.

Tom You'd very generously given up your Byron. We haven't seen them for years.

Alice About twenty.

Tom Why on earth do they want to come? I'll be busy all morning on the terrace.

Alice Actually, they're coming for dinner.

Tom *Dinner*? Are you mad? That's far worse than lunch. Why dinner? Oh God. People we haven't the faintest desire to see turning up on a Sunday night ...

Alice You're being very slightly irrational.

Tom Maybe I am. It's my feeling, nonetheless.

Alice I thought dinner would be better. We'd have the whole day to prepare.

Tom The whole day to prepare, indeed! But you've got your essay to write, you told me, urgent matter. Your *Don Juan*. The whole of Canto One, you said. That's a very long canto, I remember. And I've no doubt you've got to get ahead with your *Hamlet*.

Alice Tom. I've said I'm sorry.

Tom (*taking her empty glass*) No wonder you needed a drink. And another thing. I'm damned if I'm going to produce the sort of wine that Edward would consider drinkable.

Alice Quite.

Tom We'll drink a good bottle tonight, though, you and me. Get ourselves into a state of complete oblivion so that we don't have to think about tomorrow. You can imagine how Edward will behave, can't you? I know his sort: secretly sneering at our cellar, letting it drop he's into the seventy-eights while believing we're naïvely enjoying last year's Beaujolais ... He'll have to be dealt with.

Alice (*smiling*) As a matter of fact, it might be quite interesting, seeing them again.

Tom Doubt it. I'm never very interested in figures from the past. You're the curious one. (*He sits beside her on the sofa and puts a hand on her knee*)

Alice Good heavens! You've put your hand on my knee.

Tom You're not meant to comment upon such matters.

Alice (*pleased, looking round*) We'll have to do a lot of tidying up.

Tom As they've invited themselves, I see no reason to do any tidying up whatsoever.

Alice I'll have to get a couple of pheasants out of the deep freeze.

Tom One will do.

Alice Don't be ridiculous! You know what an enormous appetite Edward's got.

Tom (*after a pause*) I didn't know that, no.

Alice Incredible, considering how thin he was.

Tom Laura ate like a bird. Is he still thin, Edward?

Alice Very.

Tom Did you like thin men?

Alice I suppose I must have done. Edward wasn't the thinnest. You've taken your hand off my knee.

Tom Too much attention and you'll begin taking me for granted.

Alice Shall I tell you something strange? I was quite unnerved by that awful wedding.

Tom You should have stayed at home with *Don Juan* and me.

Alice I know. You're nearly always right. (*She pauses to think*) The silly thing is, I can't remember precisely what it was you did to Laura.

Tom I took her to the cinema. Several times.

Alice That was it.

Tom What could you do to a girl in a cinema in those days? No, she wasn't one of the bright stars of my past, Laura. Definitely somewhere near the bottom of the second league. Edward, on the other hand, was in your first division, I seem to remember.

Alice For a very short time.

Tom Ullswater. I remember you said it took place in Ullswater.

Alice Before it was so popular. *Ullswater* I mean. It was rather nice, then. Your memory.

Tom Good as yours.

Both smile

Perhaps you're right. Perhaps it will be interesting to see them again. Good old Laura and Edward.

Alice (*waving her drink*) At this precise moment, I feel sublimely unmoved by the whole prospect.

Tom Your sublimely unmoved moments never last. (*He looks at his watch*) Shall we abandon the potatoes?

Alice Why not?

Tom I'll make them up to you another night. (*He looks down at her, loving*) Strangely enough, you look very young in those scholarly glasses. "... Somewhere you have been sixteen and this is a loss I live with."

Alice What?

Tom Poem called "To his Love in Middle Age" by one Edwin Brock. Don't suppose he'd be in your syllabus. But a good poet. "Somewhere you have been sixteen" ——

Alice You didn't know me when I was sixteen ——

Tom "Letters, old photographs and names keep covering the tracks between us" ——

Alice Tom, are you all right?

Tom "I have stabbed all your lovers with a long knife, but lacerated only you."

Alice Actually, it's been the other way round.

Tom Stop interrupting. How does it go then? Ah. "Now jealousy winds you tight around me, already your toes and fingertips are turning blue."

Silence between them. Alice examines her fingertips

Alice Absolute rubbish, the jealousy bit, the winding tight bit. I've never known a man so lacking in jealousy. I've never known a man so utterly unminding about ... what has been. (*Pause*) And also, please note, the whiteness of my fingertips.

Alice holds out her hand, splaying the fingers. Tom moves a little towards her, scrutinizes the hand with mock seriousness, then spreads his own hand toward her. Their fingers just touch

Fade to Black-out

Scene 2

The same. Later that evening

The remains of dinner, plus two bottles of partially drunk wine have joined the general rummage on the table. There is also a large unlit candle

The Lights come up on Alice sitting on the floor, unskilfully polishing a silver candlestick. Its pair is beside her

Tom enters carrying a tray, awkwardly making room for it on the table

Tom We forgot to light the candle.

Alice That's the whole trouble with our marriage. We put a candle on the table, full of good intentions, then forget to light it.

Tom Very obscure metaphors you mature students use. Too clever for me. (*He lights the candle*) There. "Barrister bends over backwards". Bit late, but it'll help us on our way to glorious oblivion. Burn out all thoughts of tomorrow. What on earth are you doing?

Alice Polishing the candlesticks.

Tom I can see that. Not a very regular event.

Alice I thought if we're going to have dinner in the dining-room we'd better ——

Tom (*totally incredulous*) Dinner in the dining-room? What are you talking about? We haven't had dinner in the dining-room since the Christmas before last.

Alice I thought it would be safer. Unused. Less clues.

Tom You mean, you think they're coming to spy on our life?

Alice I'm not sure what I think. But I'm convinced we must be in the dining-room.

Tom Confounded nuisance, the whole thing. All this fuss. (*He bends down and picks up the other candlestick and a duster. He takes them to the sofa and starts to polish a minute area very hard*) But what puzzles me is why you lumber yourself with the extra burden of insisting on the dining-room. I mean, if you think of it, once upon a time you spent a few rainy weekends with Edward in Ullswater. I took Laura to *The African Queen*. Not much else. Now why should those two facts go against our having a perfectly ordinary dinner in here?

Alice I don't want them eating in here.

Tom sighs. He stops polishing for a moment and holds up the candlestick, admiring his work

Tom Then I stand by my wife. The dining-room it shall be.

The telephone rings. Both freeze. They look at one another, in mutual reluctance to answer it. They wait some moments, jarred

Probably to say they're not coming after all.

Alice answers it, tense. Pause

Alice Oh, Edward. ... Yes, hallo. (*Long pause, she signals vaguely at Tom*) Well, yes, I imagine that would be fine. I expect we'd love to meet her. I mean. I'm almost sure we'd love to meet her. ... You don't know her? ... Oh, you've just met her. I see. ... Well, obviously. I mean, we'll be four already, won't we? One more doesn't make that much difference, does it? An odd number is always full of more ... potential, I think. ... (*Small laugh*) Quite. We look forward to seeing you tomorrow evening, then. Bye. (*She puts down the receiver very slowly*) *You bastard!* Why did you have to be at the wedding and make me make such ludicrous suggestions? (*Turning to Tom*) That's bloody well the last straw. They're not only coming, they're bringing a complete stranger. A Mrs Dickinson. She happens to be staying in the same house. She happens to be getting a lift back to London with them. So, of course they can't very well not bring her, can they? We're going to be invaded.

Tom The inconsideration ——

Alice If I'd thought quicker, I would have said no. No, you can't bring her, I would have said. We don't want her, I would have said. We don't want any of you! None of you can come ——

Tom Alice, it's ——

Alice (*screaming*) We don't want any of them here!

Tom and Alice face each other in silence, both holding a candlestick like a weapon. Eyes locked, helpless, they don't move for a while. Eventually, Tom shrugs

Tom (*gently*) Would you like me to clear the table or carry on polishing?

Alice makes a gesture of not knowing, then visibly controls herself, a great effort to be lively

Alice (*returning to her polishing, smiling*) You know, when I saw Edward this afternoon I couldn't help remembering what might be called our break-up scene. We were sitting in his car by the Serpentine, a windy afternoon. He said: whoever you marry, whatever may happen to you, you'll always be mine.

Tom Just the sort of codswallop people come up with in the heat of the moment. (*He fills two glasses of wine from the bottle on the table, hands one to Alice*)

Alice It may be. But I don't think he's forgotten it. He gave me a proprietorial sort of look at the wedding. As if after all these years, just because we once had a mild fling, he still had some claim on me.

Tom (*taking his wine to the sofa, resuming his polishing*) My darling Alice, you're an incorrigible romantic. Your imagination does you great disservice. I know you: brilliant at understanding books, but misinterpreting real life as usual. Plainly the wretched Edward, a little startled by the somewhat,

er, mellowed face of his old flame, gave a polite smile to conceal his
surprise, a surprise none of us, I'm bound to say, can help feeling on
reacquaintance with an old friend after a long absence ... And you leap to
the conclusion ——

Alice No! You're wrong. It wasn't that. As a matter of fact, he said I hadn't
changed a bit.

Tom Well, of course he said that. Any gentleman would. Couldn't very well
say anything else, could he? I mean, he'd hardly remark on the crow's feet
round your eyes and then ask himself to dinner. We're all skilled in
hypocrisy when it's convenient. I shall probably find myself telling Laura
she hasn't changed one bit, either, tomorrow.

Alice (*mildly*) She has, actually.

Tom I'm sure she has.

Alice At least, I think she has. Certainly her waist has gone. But perhaps she
never had one. I don't remember. I hardly knew her.

Tom She had an uneventful figure, Laura. True. (*He holds up the candlestick*) Look! Our old lovers will be dazzled. I'd quite like Edward to think
we had a butler. Good for him. Think I'll talk about how we have to fend
for ourselves on a Sunday evening.

Alice smiles

Laura will probably take an interest in the terrace. She was quite keen on
gardens, I seem to remember. Going on about her little roof patch as if it
was acres of Capability Brown. Actually, she'd made it quite nice, despite
her appalling taste for red salvia.

Alice I didn't realize you did much strolling through roof gardens with Laura.
I thought you mostly went to the cinema.

Tom Mostly we did. But there was sometimes a little ... mild hanky-panky
after an evening with Bogart.

Alice Was that *on* the roof?

Tom You know me. I've told you many times. I've no memory for carnal
delights. Perhaps there weren't any. Till I met you. (*Pause*) Laura was just
a girl, far as I recall. (*He looks at Alice's face*) Funny: you've known about
every girl there ever was. A wife's privilege, that. I confessed to you at the
height of our turbulent engagement, remember, in a Wiltshire cornfield.
You persuaded me to make a list on a book of matches ——

Alice Two books of matches.

Tom If you say so. Two books of matches.

Alice (*after a pause, very quietly*) Just one name excluded.

Tom Are you forgetting our pact?

Alice No, I'm not forgetting our pact, silence so convenient to you. But I was
just trying to remember how long ago was all that?

Tom Alice ——
Alice Three years in August. Well, we survived.
Tom Exactly. We're here. We're perfectly all right. We're pretty happy.
Alice I suppose we should be thankful for that.
Tom It's amazing the human capacity for surviving storms if everyone pulls together. You behaved impeccably in the end. I stayed. I'm never going to go, now. And I love you.

Tom gets up and goes over to Alice and ruffles her hair

You're a better polisher than me, too. Wonderful.
Alice Here. Give me yours for a final go.
Tom "Barrister polishes for wife's old lover". That'd give them something to talk about in the courts. (*He passes her the candlestick and inefficiently begins to pile things on to the tray*) There's no need to be agitated about Laura. Now if I was worried about your past, why there *would* be something to worry about. The trouble with old lovers is that they jiggle about in your mind every single day, far as I can tell. For all I know, even while you're washing up, or studying your lusty Byron, what's actually going on in your head would make a jealous man weep. Memory is often much randier than real life — perhaps that's what keeps your recollections going. Dick, Harry — Edward, of course, dare say the whole grubby crowd of them are queuing up to be recycled in your memory.
Alice What nonsense you talk!
Tom Whereas me, it's so different. So boring by comparison. Whatever you may suppose, ladies I might once have dallied with do not sit on benches in my mind. The benches are bare, I promise you. All feeling dead. Most detail gone. Best of all, not the slightest interest left. No curiosity, even, as to what's become of them. Just relief they're over. Thankful for what I've got now. "Barrister turns his back". I can't put it clearer than that.
Alice I believe you. All the same, *some* picture of the past must appear in the minds of old lovers who meet after many years. There can't be nothing.
Tom Don't torment yourself. You should know that one of the Lord's great blessings was to encourage us to remember our friends in vertical positions. He was wise enough to make sure our memories of things horizontal have a very short life.
Alice Nonsense. I'm more honest than you. What do I remember before you? I remember a bedroom ceiling, its tracery of cracks becoming so familiar in an hour that I might have been lying beneath them all my life. I remember a particular shoulder, so covered in freckles, I could have sworn it was free range ... Aftershaves ... The sweet, the self important, the unsubtle ... such a kaleidoscope of aftershaves: but best of all, plain skin. Then there was that pair of executive eyes ... guilt ticking in digital silence as they glanced at a surreptitious watch by the bed ...

Tom Yes, well. You've been reading too much.
Alice And all those preliminary conversations. Explaining to each other *why*
    you're in bed in the middle of the afternoon as if you both didn't know ...
    (*She looks at Tom, and gets up*) I think we should stop now. (*She puts the
    candlesticks on the dresser*) We've done enough. (*She finishes her wine*)
    It's late, I'm tired. (*She indicates the tray*) I'll just fill the dishwasher ——
Tom No you won't. I'll do it in the morning. (*He picks up the tray*)
Alice Anyway, this time tomorrow they'll be gone. I hope they go very early.
Tom (*lifting the tray high, a small sign, suddenly, of being slightly drunk*)
    Never raise your hopes too high above other people's stations. (*He turns*)
    We were going to get drunk this evening: did we?
Alice I don't remember.

Tom takes her arm. They move to the door

Fade to Black-out

SCENE 3

The same. The next evening

*There has been some definite attempt to tidy the place up. The boxes of seeds
have been transferred to under the table*

*The Lights come up on Alice, in jeans, shaking the cushions on the sofa, trying
to find places for her books, straightening pictures. Tom is roving about with
three bottles of wine. He puts them in one place, in an exaggerated straight
line. But, dissatisfied, picks them up and lines them somewhere else*

Tom Château Sainsbury, Château Waitrose, Château Marks and Spencer.
    What d'you think?
Alice For Edward? Château Bargain Basement?
Tom Do him good to drink the same as the rest of us.

*Alice suddenly flings herself down on the sofa on the newly puffed-up
cushions*

Alice Can't think of anything else. We've done more than enough. I'm
    exhausted.
Tom (*looking at her*) Wife flops. Two pheasants was a wild extravagance.
Alice (*eyes shut, very weary*) Two pheasants is not a wild extravagance for
    five.

Tom Bloody cheek bringing this Dickinson woman. Are you going to change?

Alice Hadn't thought of it. Why?

Tom Nothing.

Alice Well then.

Tom I'd quite like you to appear more glamorous than Laura.

Alice (*smiling*) In that case I need about four minutes. (*She sits up and punches up the cushions again*) I'm not sure I'm going to be able to get through this evening.

Tom Nonsense. You arranged it.

Alice I warn you. I might run away any moment.

Tom That would be cowardly and churlish. Not like you.

The doorbell rings

There they are.

Alice I was thinking ... you know what I was thinking? That it must be very difficult for people who've had famous lovers. Ministers, authors, cricket captains — smiling away at you on television night after night ... Imagine a Chancellor of the Exchequer! He'd be worst of all, waving his little red box. You couldn't help thinking it, it wasn't his little red box he waved at *me* ...

The doorbell rings again

Tom You arranged it, you go.

Alice (*getting up*) You wanted me to change.

Tom opens his mouth to abuse, but is cut off by a devastating smile from his wife

"Barrister behaves beautifully".

Alice exits. Tom exits to the front door

There is the murmur of two men's voices

Tom enters followed by Edward. Edward carries a bottle of wine behind his back

Tom Here we are. Now.

Edward Well. Sorry about the womenfolk. They shouldn't be too long. (*Pause. He hands the bottle to Tom*) Small contribution.

Tom Oh really, good heavens. You shouldn't have. (*He takes the bottle. Trying to conceal amazement*) Latour nineteen seventy ... My dear Edward. Not sure I can compete with that. Thanks most awfully.

Edward (*shrugging*) I'm in the business.

Tom So Alice was saying. Very top of the business, she said.

Edward (*modest*) Well, you know how it is. Chairman, as a matter of fact. Family firm — not my family, which makes one's position more satisfactory. (*Pause*) One progresses.

Tom Quite. Now. A drink, a drink, a drink. Glass of wine or something else?

Tom watches Edward glance along the row of Sainsbury's, etc.

Edward Gin, I think, please.

Tom Quite. Safest gin. (*Going to the drinks tray*) Sorry about no Alice. Always leaves changing to the last minute. Always optimistic about time being on her side. She's never learned it never is. Darling Alice, terribly unpunctual, as you probably ... Well ...

Edward Punctuality, to my mind, is one of life's great dividers. The unpunctual should never marry the punctual if they want a long and happy life, don't you think?

Tom Something in that. (*He hands Edward the drink*)

Edward Thanks, lovely. Laura, I'm proud to say, is always on the dot.

Tom (*flat*) Is she.

Edward On the *dot*. Course, I dare say one of the pleasures for unpunctual partners is all that waiting about for each other — hours in stations, restaurants, cars. No apologies when they finally meet. Complete understanding. No regret at time wasted. Extraordinary.

Tom (*laughing politely*) Quite a thought. (*He picks up the Latour*) I say, shall we have this with the pheasant?

Edward That was my hope.

Tom Then I'd better open it. (*He sets about this with much care. Eventually he stands it in the row beside the other bottles*)

Edward (*looking about*) Pretty nice set-up you've got here.

Tom Set-up?

Edward Well, I mean, room, place, house.

Tom Oh, I see. I always think set-up sounds a bit illegal. Well, yes. It's coming on after twenty years. We're in the process of making a terrace, matter of fact.

Edward Really? Laura will be interested.

Tom Thought she might be.

Edward She's a great little gardener.

Tom I remember her roof garden in Ashley Place. Very impressive.

Edward I never saw that. Before my day.

Tom Very hot on filipendula hexapetala, she was.

Edward (*faintly nervous*) Is that ...?

Tom Common old dropwort, actually. Never liked it myself.

Edward (*laughing*) I always think some of those Latin names sound like ... well you know.

Tom (*really laughing*) How right you are! Never thought of that. (*He thinks*) Juniperus horizontalis. Martensia virginia. Lingus vulgare. Good God, you could be prosecuted for any of them. (*He starts whirling about and laughing*)

When both stop laughing, Tom stops whirling about, stands and openly contemplates Edward

How long is it?

Edward How long is ...? Oh, twenty-one years.

Tom *Twenty-one years?*

Edward Longish time.

Tom Very. I say, I'm sorry about no Alice.

Edward Oh, she'll be down. I'm enjoying the anticipation. I hope it hasn't ... A Sunday evening ...

Tom No, no, not at all. Though you'll have to take us as we are. No help on a Sunday and all that.

Edward Laura thought it would be a wonderful opportunity.

Tom So did Alice, apparently.

Edward It was rather amusing, running into each other like that. I happened to look across the room and what do I see but a feather-hatted figure standing on a chair. I thought: that can't be anyone but Alice! I helped her down, as a matter of fact.

Tom Oh, it was you who helped her down?

Edward Years ago, you know, I used to tease Alice. One day you'll be a proper eccentric, Alice, I used to say: you'll be an eccentric old lady.

Tom (*after a slight pause, defensive*) Standing up on a chair is hardly an eccentric act if you feel the need to look down, see who's there, is it? If I ——

Edward I wasn't suggesting ——

Tom I mean if I felt inclined to look down on something, I'd be very likely to get up on something ——

Edward Look, don't get me wrong. Of course I didn't mean Alice ——

Tom Tell you what, I'll give her a call.

Edward I don't mean Alice is eccentric *now*, just because ——

Tom goes to the door and opens it

Tom (*shouting*) Alice!

Silence

She'll be having a devil of a job choosing her jewellery.

Edward (*surprised*) She's acquired a taste for jewellery, has she? I never thought she liked jewellery.

Tom My dear fellow, what woman, actually confronted by diamonds, can resist? You know how it is. (*Pause*) One progresses. Who's this woman you're bringing with you?

Edward Sorry about that. We couldn't get out of it. She asked for a lift. Mary Dickinson. Rather striking.

Tom Ah, well. One more can't make much difference to two pheasants. (*He sweeps up the three supermarket bottles of wine. Small laugh to himself*) "Barrister boobs badly". Think I'll just go and upgrade the back-up bottles. Help yourself to another drink.

Tom exits fast

Edward, alone, feels himself to be in a peculiar sort of place. He travels curiously about the room, tops up his drink, swoops on to Alice's books, picks up and inspects a copy of Byron, glances at her notes. Then he comes across her glasses. He picks them up, examines them in some wonderment

Alice enters quietly behind him. At first he does not see her. Alice has tried hard. She looks marvellous in a black satin safari suit and diamond earrings. Unobserved, she studies Edward's back view for a moment

Alice (*softly*) Edward!

Edward, disguising a start, turns guiltily from her books. They look at each other for a long silent moment

Edward Hallo, Teasle.

Alice (*stiffening*) I don't think that's very appropriate. Not now.

Edward (*shrugging*) Sorry. It's hard to think of you as Alice.

Alice Well, I am Alice. You managed to call me Alice yesterday, at the wedding.

Edward I know how to behave in public.

Alice Where are Laura and the woman you've brought?

Edward They said it was such a lovely evening they wanted to walk the last bit. I dropped them off at the crossroads. They'll be here in a minute.

Alice Who's the woman?

Edward I don't know much about her except that she hasn't been married long. Her husband's abroad.

Alice Pretty cheeky, foisting herself upon you. Still, I suppose one neutral party might make things easier.

Edward I don't think things will be that difficult, will they? We're all grown up.

Alice Where's Tom?

Edward Dealing with the wine.

Alice glances at the bottle of Latour, goes over to it

Alice (*picking it up*) Did you bring this?

Edward Small contribution. I thought ——

Alice Very grand present. Thank you. (*Pause*) You've come a long way from that Spanish stuff we used to drink.

Edward smiles. Alice folds her arms, scrutinizes him with amusement

I always knew you'd end up at the top of something or other. You were always so totally, utterly inflamed by ambition. Determined to succeed, as they say.

Edward Me?

Alice (*smiling*) You had exactly the right priorities for a man who wants to get to the top. Everything came second to ambition. You thought there was absolutely nothing wrong, for instance, in cutting short an ... assignment to get to a meeting. And how right you were! Here you are now, a managing director. (*She pours herself a drink*)

Edward Chairman, actually.

Alice That's wonderful.

Edward Teasle. Alice. My waspish old thing. I'm hardly through the door and you're on the attack.

Alice (*looking up, slightly flirtatious*) You mean, I haven't changed?

Edward (*after a long pause*) No.

Alice (*pleased*) Really?

Edward Not as far as I can see. Not in essentials.

Alice slinks over to the sofa, flings herself down and crosses her legs, faintly provocative. She picks up the book Edward has recently put down

Alice (*quietly*) No opportunity to judge the essentials this evening. (*Small smile*) Outward appearances are all you can go by.

Edward Then I judge them ... pretty good.

Alice Anyhow. I bet you something. I bet you never imagined your waspish old thing would end up with letters after her name.

Edward No! Good heavens! I'd no idea. I'm sorry. I never read the Honours List ——

Alice Not that! BA. Serious letters. (*She waves the book*) Quite soon, all being well.

Edward I'm most impressed.

Alice So you see, I'm not just a wife, mother and desirable sex object after all.

Edward I never thought you would be.

Alice No. Well, I'm not. (*She drinks*) Any year now I'll be able to call myself an intellectual.

Edward I'm glad to see you can still laugh at yourself. (*He gets up, fetches her glasses and hands them to her*) I'd like to see you in your glasses.

Alice (*putting them on, posing for him*) All right?

Edward Beautiful.

Tom enters, shuffling fast, carrying two dusty bottles of Latour. With a great show of understatement, he puts them beside Edward's bottle

Tom turns to Alice, whose pose has crumpled and Edward, who tries to disguise amazement at Tom's bottles

Tom Can't quite match your year but they're not bad. (*Taking in Alice*) Good Lord! "Barrister boggles"! You've got yourself up a bit. (*To Edward*) Sunday nights, butler out, we usually stay as we are.

Alice and Edward exchange a look that Tom does not see

Alice Tom!

Tom (*putting on a nearby jacket, doing up his collar and finding a crumpled tie in the pocket*) Tell you what I was thinking. I was thinking Edward might like to see the terrace — what there is of it — before dinner. At this rate, Laura'll have to see it by moonlight. But I'd like Edward to get a glance before it's dark. Alice?

Alice (*brightly*) I'll come. Edward?

Edward Of course.

Tom Bring your drink.

They all begin to move towards the french windows. Tom puts a hand on Edward's shoulder

You'll have to understand, of course, there's still a long way to go. But I dare say a man of your vision will see the potential. This time next year I'm hoping the whole thing will be shipshape and we'll have enjoyed a summer of eating al fresco among the calluna vulgaris ... (*He laughs*) Or whatever. Mind the step.

Tom, Edward and Alice exit

A moment of absolute silence. Then the bell rings. Voices off. Footsteps

Laura and Mary enter. Laura, pleasant looking but faded, has greying hair and no interest in fashion. Mary is rather elegant, in trousers, boots, silk shirt and jacket, Herbert Johnson hat, severe. She looks about, curious

Laura (*calling*)Hallo! This is rather nice. I wonder if they're outside. (*She goes to the french windows, peers out*) There they are. Tom! Alice! Edward's taking a pretend interest in the roses. Extraordinary.

Mary You can't ever be certain, but guessing history from signs is irresistible. My line of country really — archaeology.

Laura (*impressed*) Archaeology! Goodness me.

Mary Putting the past together from clues. (*As she moves about she touches things, curious*) It's rather intriguing trying to do the same with the present.

Laura Oh, what fun! Well, from the clues here, I would guess that Tom and Alice have an exceptionally happy marriage, like Edward and me.

Mary gives Laura a look. They both hear footsteps on the terrace outside. Mary quickly moves to the bookshelves, where she will have her back to Tom when he comes in

Tom enters, bounding exuberantly

He leaps upon Laura who becomes quite skittish in her pleasure at seeing him

Tom My dearest Laura Dora! This is a treat!

Laura Tom!

Tom Marvellous! Here, let's have a look at you.

Tom pushes Laura a little away from him, taking her in

Laura It's been so long. (*She looks him up and down, appraising*)

Tom It has too. Far too long.

Laura You've not changed.

Tom (*modest*) Oh, I don't know. (*He pats his stomach. His eyes trail to Mary's back view*) This is ...?

Mary turns slowly, meets his eye. Tom's expression is blank, pale

Laura (*squeezing his arm*) Sorry, this is Mary Dickinson. Tom Adderly.

Tom and Mary move towards each other, shake hands

Tom How do you do.

Mary This is very good of you.

Laura Tom, I insist on seeing the garden before the light goes.

Tom (*heavy*) We'll all go. Let me get you a drink first.

Laura When we come back will do me. (*She is poised eagerly at the french windows*)

Tom I'll just get one for Mrs Dickinson.

Laura exits

(*He goes to the window. Shouting after her*) You'll find Edward and Alice down by the roses. (*He turns to Mary*) *What the hell are you doing here?*

Mary Promises! You promised ——

Tom shuts the french window. He turns slowly towards Mary. He looks at her in absolute, incredulous silence. Mary smiles. Tom fights for words. He picks up a bottle of whisky as if it was a weapon

Tom (*beginning fast, but quietly, suppressing his fury*) I suppose you want your usual bourbon on the rocks, as you so grandly used to call it after your two weeks in New York? (*Beginning to lose control*) Well we don't have bourbon, so you'll have to have Haig.

Mary (*quietly*) I don't drink bourbon any more.

Tom (*stumped for a moment*) Oh. (*Beginning to roar again*) I told you I never wanted to see you again, ever.

Mary You also promised me ——

Tom Stop going on about promises!

Mary I'd have thought that as a barrister, a man of honour, you ——

Tom You're a woman of experience! You should know by now that promises are unreliable cement between changing circumstances. (*He pours the drink furiously*) Circumstances changed.

Mary (*cool*) I see.

Tom Why in God's name did you come?

Mary It was an irresistible opportunity ——

Tom Always a snatcher of opportunities. There's no more ice and I'm damned if I'm going to get you any. (*He holds out the drink*)

Mary — to see you. To see how you were.

Tom (*with relish*) Still hate iceless whisky, do you?

Mary I do, thanks. (*She takes the glass and moves away*)

Tom I don't understand. How did you get here?

Mary Does it matter? Three years, waiting patiently, then my chance comes.

Tom What are you hoping to do?

Mary I thought you might have mellowed.

Tom Well you were wrong. I have not mellowed. You'd better go. Get out. Quickly. Before they come back.

Mary Did you get my letters?

Tom Get out!

Mary Did you? Weren't you the slightest bit moved by my reasoning?

Tom I said go. Now! Or I'll ——

Mary What will you do? I can't possibly go now. What would they say?

Tom I'll think of something. Just get out. Leave me alone.

Mary Stop shouting at me! Where's your sense of humour?

Tom Humour? This doesn't strike me as a very humorous situation.

Mary My presence seems to disturb you. Interesting.

Tom (*wiping his handkerchief shakily over his brow*) I'm fully in control.

Mary I came because ——

Tom You only came because as usual you've no consideration for anyone else's life.

Mary Was that how it seemed to you?

Tom Demands, demands — ridiculous demands you made. Absurd hopes you lived on! When? you kept asking. Never, I said a million times. You should have believed me. I begged you to believe me. But no. Vain as ever, you thought you'd win.

Mary You never used to be like this, so condemning.

Tom Nothing's changed. Understand?

Mary (*bitter laugh*) Nothing's changed for me, either. Christ I understand. You said you'd be in touch in a year or so. You weren't. I'm fed up with waiting, Tom. Why should you get away with it so easily?

Tom For God's sake. All right, I may have made imprudent promises. You know how it is. Desire spurs hopeless visions, impractical plans ——

Mary Desire? It was only desire, was it?

Tom I may have asked you in the heat of the ... I only promised ... Hell, I can't remember what I promised.

Mary You behaved rottenly. I remember that. I, on the other hand, apart from goading you a little through the post, behaved rather well, don't you think? I knew where you lived. I could have called and made a scene at any time. But I've resisted — three years. Anyway, now I'm here at last and I'm staying for the evening.

Tom Oh!

Mary Tom. You're quite capable of going through with it.

Tom I don't want to go through with it. I don't want to go through anything with you ever again — least of all some lunatic deception. (*Pause*) Please go.

Mary You know I've got to stay, unless you want them to think something very peculiar is going on. Don't worry. I will behave myself. (*Deliberately seductive, she undoes her hair and tosses it about. She smiles at Tom as she goes towards him, holding out her empty glass*) I need another drink.

Tom seeing this, is thrown. We see the fight ebbing from him. He takes her glass in slow motion

Tom Why are you suddenly Mrs Dickinson?

Mary I got married two years, almost to the day, after you so gallantly dropped me in Epping Forest and drove off for ever.

Beat, while they look at each other

Tom So, what do you want?

Mary You owe me explanations. You promised me that if ever things at home changed ——

Tom (*snapping*) Well they haven't. (*He turns away so that Mary shall not see his face*) Alice and I are very happy. We've been happy for years.

Mary The old refrain ... Were you so happy with Alice when you and I were together?

Tom You never understood, did you? A man doesn't have to be unhappy with his wife to be attracted — deeply attracted — to another woman.

Mary Ah!

Tom I love my wife. (*He sighs*) This is typical of you, giving in to lethal curiosity, no thought of the consequences. (*Very quietly*) This is a foolish, selfish thing to do, Mrs Dickinson. Bloody mad. Treacherous.

Mary I'd hoped by now we could relate in a new perspective. Maybe I miscalculated.

Tom Christ! Where did you pick up this social worker language? You certainly miscalculated! It was going to have been perfectly all right, this evening, living out my wife's absurd invitation, getting through it dutifully. But you've put an end to all that.

Mary (*smiling sweetly at Tom, sitting*) For so long I'd been looking for a way of meeting without causing too much chaos — the fury of a broken heart doesn't fade. After three years, chance came my way, Elizabeth's wedding, just a few miles from here. I thought, Tom's bound to be there. But you weren't. God, though, was on my side. The Harrisons, complete strangers to me, staying in the same house for the wedding. They offered me a lift back to London. They'd arranged to have dinner with Tom and Alice Adderly. Do I know them? Not at all, I say, flesh going cold. We're sure they won't mind one more, they say — My chance! My chance, Tom. I never imagined we'd have a moment alone.

Tom (*sarcastic*) Did you suppose in your madness that I might have said: that's it, Mig. Let's be off?

Mary (*reacting to her nickname*) I suppose I hoped for something like that.

Tom Any thoughts for your happily married husband, or didn't he come into your calculations?

Mary I would have left him. He wouldn't have been surprised. In such imperfect situations, there have to be victims.

Long pause. Incredulous, Tom shakes his head

Tom What sort of a woman are you now? I used to think I knew.

Mary One who loves absolutely.

Tom Absolute love can only destroy.

Mary You called me Mig!

Tom Old habit. (*Reflecting, almost to himself*) You and Alice there at the wedding, unknown to each other. To think of that! She came back with some spiel about a golden thread linking people — people innocent of its devious directions. (*Small laugh*) Even looking down from her chair she could — never have seen the greatest irony of all ...

Mary What are you talking about?

Tom Doesn't matter. (*Looking nervously at her rather determined stance*) Hope you haven't come here bent on destruction.

Mary Grant me some restraint. There was something I refrained from putting in a letter.

Pause

Tom What was that?

Mary (*grasping her drink*) Soon after you left I found I was pregnant.

Mary takes in Tom's appalled reaction with some relish

Tom Christ, Mig. (*He sits down beside her*) What on earth ——?

Mary (*bitter laugh*) It turned out to be a phantom pregnancy — just my luck. Case of profound wish-fulfilment. Nothing messy. A sort of nervous breakdown, that's all. Against all my better judgement, I found myself going to a psychiatrist ——

Tom I'm so sorry. If it had been real, I would of course have ——

Mary — paid the school fees. I'm sure you would. I have to admit, he did help — the psychiatrist. He listened so profoundly while I trawled through it all, and in some respects I'm fine, now.

Tom Psychiatrist, phantom pregnancy ... I'd no idea ... how awful, Mig. It must have been dreadful, going through it alone, though God knows how I could have helped. But you're a strong woman. I've always admired your strength. It wasn't easy, not answering your letters, I can tell you.

Mary I still love you.

Tom (*helpless*) Oh dear. The mess of it all.

Mary The affection I feel for my husband is in a different league from what I feel for you. But I'm grateful to him. He's a very kind man, Professor Dickinson.

Tom *Professor* Dickinson?

Mary Yes, I married my psychiatrist.

Tom Good God. Things must have been bad. Very old syndrome, of course: patient into wife. Suppose he knows you pretty well. You can pack in a lot of history at fifty pounds an hour ——

Mary No need to sneer. We're content in our way. He stabilized me.

Tom Stabilized? Is he the man responsible for your ghastly new vocabulary?

Mary He knows I think of you much of the time and he accepted that.

Tom How very lucky for him.

Mary I married him out of need for a guide, a support. But you're the only man I've ever loved so deeply that I couldn't ... account for my actions.

Tom Is that a threat? Please Mig, don't upset things now. Not after so long.

Mary (*bitter laugh*) Upset things? For you, you mean. Things have been very upset for *me*. The kind of love I'm talking about, prohibited, can ruin a life.

Tom Please, please, let's not go over it all again. You know I could never leave Alice, the children. All this. Sweet familiarity of house and garden ... Sevatolina not yet planted, whole herbaceous plan still a little hazy in my mind. But a phantom pregnancy, dear God ... Enough to crack a man's hardened heart.

Mary (*sadly, bravely*) Even a phantom child of yours, for the short time it lived, was some consolation.

Tom (*shutting his eyes*) Don't, Mig.

When Tom opens his eyes he sees a sudden shift of spirits in Mary: a gaiety

Mary Know what I'd like to do right this minute? (*She moves closer to him*)

Tom Mig, please ——

Mary Come on!

She kisses him quickly on the mouth. He pushes her away. Mary shrugs, good humoured

We were used to so little time, weren't we? (*She laughs*) We almost thrived on it, remember?

Forcefully, she kisses him again. Tom submits for a moment

There! There's my proof! You couldn't kiss me like that if you didn't still love me ...

Tom Stop confusing me!

Mary kisses his hands in turn

I've succeeded so well in putting you almost completely out of my mind. Now here you are, ungrounding me again, damn you. Please stop, Mig. This is dangerous.

Mary (*delighted*) You can't deny that you didn't love it when I ...

She runs a finger from his knee, up his body, to his mouth. She leaves it there a second while he almost imperceptibly kisses it. Then again pushes her away

Tom No!

Mary (*pleased by his shaken reaction*) Very well. If I'm really alarming you. (*Beat*) Never for one moment, you know, have I forgotten anything. Oh God, I love you, Tom ——

Tom Please don't keep saying that. I can't think straight at the moment. I don't really want to think. (*He pulls himself together*) But the immediate thing is this evening. We've got to get through this evening. If Alice ever knew ...

Mary Surely she wouldn't mind about something so long past?

Tom Not that long past, and you don't know Alice. She's always surprised how I discount what's over. To her, the past is always dancing, threatening, haunting. I see it in her eyes, a daily ghost.

Mary You never told her anything about me?

Tom Not a thing. How could I? She just knew there was someone. Some sort of crisis I kept to myself. A terrible threat, she imagined. But she never knew your name. She knows everything about every one before we were married. You were my only bit of unofficial infidelity as it were. She wanted to be spared the details, naturally ... (*He gets up, strides to the french windows, looks out, returns*) They must have gone round the kitchen garden. Boring Edward to death in the cabbage patch. Serve him right. (*Small laugh*)

Mary (*after a silence*) Is Laura an old girlfriend?

Tom Of a minor order. I was thinking, she's aged a bit. I don't know when her prime was — certainly not at the time of our brief affair.

Mary She looks like one of those women whose prime is perpetually on the wane ——

Tom You beast!

Mary And very conventional for you.

Tom Didn't used to be, far as I remember. She once wore black nail polish on her toes. Bought it at a joke shop. (*He chuckles*) "I'm very before my time," she said, "you'll see." And sure enough my daughter wore the same ghastly stuff, a few years back, her first term at Durham. But you, Mig, are you still working hard as ever? Digging round the world? Still having problems with digging groupies?

Mary (*smiling*) Still digging for my favours, I'm glad to say. It's become
sexual harassment since I last saw you, hasn't it? But I always rather enjoy
the passes in the heat and dust. The day they stop — I'll know my pulling
power has come to an end.

Tom That won't be for ... Mig, you've got to behave impeccably tonight you
know.

Mary I'll hardly open my mouth. I'll do my best. (*Smiling, she pulls a thin
gold chain pendant from under her shirt. She holds it out from her neck*)
Remember this? (*She laughs*) You bought it from the souvenir shop on the
cross Channel ferry.

Tom Day trip to Calais! We were driven to such things.

Mary Rough crossing. March wind.

Tom April, surely?

Mary You leant over the side and said you'd rather throw yourself in than
lose me.

Tom Did I?

Mary (*picking up Tom's hand and sandwiching it between her own and her
bosom*) I never take it off.

Tom Don't Mig. (*He pulls his hand away gently*) I've scrubbed almost
everything from my memory ——

Mary Except Laura's nail polish!

Tom The sort of inconsequential nonsense that sticks.

Mary (*holding out the pendant*) And this? This sort of nonsense that sticks?

Tom You must be the judge of that.

Mary You should be faithful to the past, you know. Most people aren't and
it's very mean. Many things go wrong — like us — and you feel sour later.
But that's no reason to forget how good it was at the time.

Tom I don't forget ... how good it was with you. That's been the trouble. I
wish to God I could. (*He looks at her, anguished*) Oh Mig ... you're thinner.

Mary Ah! You remember me fatter?

Tom (*confused*) Yes ... no. I remember that afternoon. Where were we? You
were walking a little ahead of me, that blue cloak you used to wear
billowing about you, flecked with snow. Some sort of lightning seemed to
strike, blindingly, though you were only talking about the time of your next
train. The four-fifteen, it was, changing at Reading. And when I kissed you,
the snow on your cheeks and in your hair melted instantly, but more snow
danced down to whiten you again. Strange rhythm for a Tuesday afternoon
— kissing, melting, snowing. Kissing, melting ——

*Footsteps. Mary puts away the pendant. Tom quickly moves farther from her,
nervous, trying to comfort himself*

Here's Alice.

Alice enters, hurrying, carrying a bunch of parsley

Alice Back now! Hallo.
Tom Ah, darling! This is Mrs Dickinson.

Mary and Alice shake hands, both smiling

Mary Mary. Hello. Funny we didn't run into each other in the scrum
yesterday. This is so ——
Alice Well, I'm so glad Edward and Laura were able to bring you. I'm one
of those people who's terribly easy about numbers. Twelve, even twenty-
four, at the last minute — nothing fazes me, does it, darling? (*To Tom*)
Tom I was just telling Mrs Dickinson ——
Mary Do call me Mary, please.
Tom I was just telling Mary ——
Alice (*to Tom*) I must tell you, Edward was being absolutely *heroic* about
your chrysanthemums ——
Tom Was he?
Alice Simply heroic, thinking of something new to say about each one. (*To
Mary*) So sweet, when you think he hates gardens with an absolute passion.
Anyhow, I'm just going to shove this over the taramasalata and we'll be
ready. Could you give them a shout? Say two minutes.

Alice exits

Mary (*going to stand close to him, quietly*) You were saying ... (*She smiles
shyly*) Kissing, melting, snowing ——
Tom (*brusquely*) Could you go and find the others? They'll be round to the
left and through the gate.

Mary exits

*Tom is alone for a few moments,. He picks up Edward's wine and a bottle of
his own, compares them with a slight smile*

Alice enters

Alice I've found a new quick way with parsley! I just pushed the stalks into
the taramasalata so it looks like a little pink desert island with a clump of
trees. Darling ... Tom?
Tom (*smiling, just*) Lovely.
Alice You're rather overdoing the wine, aren't you?
Tom I wouldn't have thought so, not on this occasion.

Alice Very generous of Edward. Very generous of you.

Tom We're very generous men.

Alice (*putting a hand on his arm*) What's the matter? You look a bit "barrister battered".

Tom (*mock cheerful*) No, no. More "barrister bowled over by wife in black satin".

Alice (*pleased*) "Barrister bearing up" then?

Tom Good heavens, yes. It's all going to be fine. Endless dull wine talk from Edward and garden talk from Laura.

Alice (*smiling, picking up Mary's hat and putting it on*) Oh, I say, I like this! Is it Mrs Dickinson's hat? I think she might be quite an asset after all.

Fade to Black-out

CURTAIN

ACT II

Scene 1

The same. Later that evening

The kitchen is dim, some of the lights turned off. Off stage there are sounds of laughter and animated voices, then of a door shutting so the voices are cut off

Alice enters followed by Laura. Alice carries a bottle of wine. Laura's glass is almost empty. Laura is ill at ease and looks to see if the others are following. Alice goes about turning on lights. She is aware of Laura's awkwardness but will make no concessions to it

Laura (*eventually*) She seemed to have a lot in common with Edward.

Alice Kind of woman who makes it her business to have a lot in common with most men. (*She bangs a cushion hard*)

Laura I think she's rather nice, rather sad and earnest. They often go together. (*She sits on the sofa*)

Alice I think she's fairly nice.

She turns on Laura whose unease has forced her into a holy-looking position. Her hands are clasped

Interesting, what Edward was saying about God. Is he religious?

Laura (*startled*) Er, no. Well, I mean yes, in the way most people are. I mean, we don't go to church much. Just Christmas ——

Alice } (*together*) — and weddings and funerals.
Laura }

Laura Are you and Tom ... churchgoers, then?

Alice We don't go often now.

Laura Oh, I do sympathize.

Alice Poor old Church of England. It's making a terrible fool of itself. Do sit down. The other day we had a serious invitation to a wine and cheese party in the graveyard. As for women priests — what do you think about them?

Laura Well, I personally ——

Alice Do you know what I saw the other day? *Priestesses*, as I shall call them, posing for the fashion pages of a serious Sunday paper. Slipping out of their jeans into loose little cassocks for the photographer — no doubt praying he would choose their best profile.

Laura Well, I personally ——

Alice Unbelievable. In future, I shall talk to God at home. (*Pause*) Your friend was very quiet at dinner.

Laura I suppose she was. She's not really a friend.

Alice (*sitting beside Laura on the sofa*) Not a contributor. In fact, I would say, verging on the penetratingly dull, as well as earnest. Terrible affliction of modern life, earnestness, particularly bad case of it among Open University students. I'm the only one who ever smiles. I think it would be fair to say Mrs Dickinson is the sort of woman who makes you feel quite tired the moment she comes through the door.

Behind them, Mary suddenly appears. She listens with a slight smile

Alice and Laura are unaware of her presence

Before she's even opened her mouth.

Slowly Mary approaches. She holds an empty glass

Laura She's not very ... no. But quite elegant.

Mary grimaces with mock surprise, pleasure. She flicks at her jacket

Mary Hall-ooo! So this is where you are. (*We can just perceive she has drunk a certain amount at dinner*)

Laura (*spinning round, deeply embarrassed to see Mary*) Mary!

Alice, amused, fills Laura's glass with more wine

(*To Alice, very confused, giggling*) Goodness. We usually go on to something less exotic after dinner.

Alice (*sweetly*) Do you?

Mary May I?

Mary thrusts her glass towards Alice. Their eyes meet, hold, for a long moment. Then Alice pours a third of a glass

Thanks. (*Beginning to amble about the room, taking it in with peculiar concentration; grimly*) Such fun, this, Alice. Such a good dinner, that was.

Alice (*brusquely*) Good. Glad you enjoyed it. My entire fantasy world is concerned about not having to think about food. To me, the worst thing about marriage is the relentless chase of meals ——

Laura Really? I rather like cooking, thinking up things for Edward. He's so appreciative.

Alice (*giving Laura a scathing look*) The constant, crushing, boring thought — what can we have for dinner today? Food, bloody food, daily.

Mary (*small laugh*) You can't be serious about it being the worst thing about marriage?

Alice Well. Few things are more serious.

Laura giggles

Mary I would have thought ... all sorts of things. The rusting of libidos, for instance. (*Her eyes lock with Alice's again*) But then I haven't been married for as long as you. Could I ...?

Alice Upstairs. Second on the right.

Mary, aware Alice's and Laura's eyes are hard upon her, exits

If you hadn't run into her, it would have been a very different sort of evening.

Laura Sorry, I ——

Alice (*impatient*) Never mind. Do you work?

Laura I'm afraid I don't, no. I'm just a wife really. Whole-time occupation. Not even any children.

Alice Then we don't have to talk about the children. That's a relief.

Laura But you've got two? Grown up?

Alice Yes, and I love my children very much. But I don't like to risk boring people with their news.

Laura I'd never be bored by your children! Tom said at dinner they were both at university ... (*Seeing Alice has no intention of elaborating*) And you — doing the Open University — that's very impressive. I could never stick the course. What's your subject?

Alice (*bored*) Humanities.

Laura Humanities? (*Long silence. She doesn't understand but refrains from asking*) I could never see myself going in for anything like that. I wonder if the others ...?

Alice I'll get them in a moment.

Laura (*taking several sips of wine as if for boldness*) Anyway ... it's nice to have a chance to meet you properly after all these years. As a matter of fact, I have to admit, I was pretty terrified of the idea.

Alice Really? Why?

Laura From what I've always gathered from Edward ... we're on a completely different plane.

Alice Probably we are. That's not to say my plane is superior to yours or vice versa. (*Gleefully*) Am I terrifying?

Laura (*small smile*) A little. I mean, I get the feeling I could never interest you.

Alice Oh, I don't know. I'd be quite interested to know how you can look so contented, just being a wife. I envy you that. It must be a much more peaceful state than mine.

Laura Something I can't explain. (*Pause*) Edward said ... you were one of the great loves of his life.

Alice Trick of memory there, I think. There was no great passion.

Laura Really?

Alice More, lustful convenience. Edward had been ditched by some girl. I was fed up with some man. We found we shared a slight enthusiasm for walking in the Lake District ——

Laura (*incredulous, indignant*) *Walking?* But Edward never goes out of the house except to get in the car! In twenty years I've never heard him mention the Lake District or any desire whatever to go there ——

Alice A man has to keep something from his wife.

Laura *Walking!* I would never have believed it.

Alice Only a passing phase, perhaps. Don't fret yourself. I seem to remember once we'd got the boots, the rucksacks and maps, our keenness was soon spent.

Laura I mean, I just can't imagine it. But then I suppose you can never know everything about someone's past, can you? Little bits keep coming out over the years, of course. But a lot doesn't, does it? You can never get the entire picture. But walking? (*She drinks*) Anyhow, here's my opportunity. I can ask you at last. I can ask you ... what was Edward like, when you and he ... ?

Alice (*pretending to think*) Do you mean what was Edward like in bed, or in general?

Mary enters, glass almost empty again

Mary I can see you two are having ... I'll just ... slip through ... don't want to disturb ...

Mary exits towards the dining-room

Laura (*very embarrassed*) What I meant was, of course, what was he like in general? I don't suppose he's changed much otherwise. Unless you managed to bring something out of him I've never experienced ...

Alice What was Edward like?

Her smile unnerves Laura

Ah! (*She sighs with mock nostalgia*) What Edward definitely was not ... was a mistake. No I remember him with great affection. His singleness of purpose would be heard to forget. I saw him as an energetic little cox ——

Laura A what ...?

Alice I mean the boat kind. I used to think of him in a small craft, negotiating the hazardous waters of professional know-how.

Laura Edward a rowing man? I've never pictured him ——

Alice As for his private life, women weren't much more to him than useful accessories. Once their usefulness was over they were, well, beached.

Laura I'm glad to say that's all in the past. These days, you couldn't find a more steadfast husband.

Alice Of course, he was young. Immature but very sweet. He had his qualities. He was never late, never too serious except about wine. He loved detail — a bit of a fusser. Then he was the only man I ever knew who kept constant bittermints in the glove compartment and wore monogrammed vests. Does that tell you anything? I expect he's changed a lot.

Laura (*thinking*) He's gone off the bittermints but the ambition's still the same, I suppose. Not that there's anywhere much further for him to go.

Alice Quite.

Laura (*trying to assess Alice*) I expect you're equally curious to know how Tom was, in our day?

Alice I'm not wildly curious, no.

Laura We shared a great love of horticulture.

Alice (*smiling sweetly*) So I understand.

Laura I mean, I only had a little roof garden in those days but he was always very encouraging.

Alice He's usually pretty encouraging, Tom. (*Pause*) That is, unless encouragement is inconvenient. If there's something he wants done and I want to work, then naturally he doesn't encourage me in my own pursuits quite so hard.

Laura Men!

Alice They don't understand that the art of being obliging is to oblige not merely when it suits *them*, but when it suits *us*. Otherwise the whole point of the kind act is lost. Here he is at last.

Tom enters

Tom Sorry, sorry. We got bogged down in the Third World. Seems some relation of Mary's in charge of a butter mountain. I was trying to envisage the job. What does a butter mountain keeper actually *do*, I wondered? Visit the butter every day watching it grow? Mary didn't seem to know.

Alice gets up, begins collecting ashtrays and empty glasses. Tom sits in the place left by Alice

It's very difficult, envisaging other people's jobs.

Off stage, there is the sound of laughter

Alice gives a look at Tom and Laura then exits with the ashtrays and glasses

Laura (*nervous*) It's been fascinating, meeting Alice properly at last.
Tom (*sitting beside Laura*) Curiosity sated, what? She's a good woman, Alice. I married the right woman. I wouldn't be married to anyone else in the world despite all the competition from Byron and Co.
Laura She's wonderful.
Tom Keeps me on my toes.
Laura I can imagine.
Tom (*putting a hand on her knee, unthinking*) Did you marry the right man?
Laura Edward? Of course.
Tom Good, good. He seems a splendid fellow. Can't think why we haven't seen you for so long. Though I suppose we have little in common except our small skirmishes in the past. (*He looks at her*) Amazing how we all get on, don't you think? Judging by this evening.
Laura Not all that amazing, really, if you think. Perhaps now the ice is broken, you and Alice will come to dinner with us? Our house is nothing like this, but quite nice for London.
Tom Of course, why not? Backwards and forwards, backwards and forwards, from now on I can see endless invitations, a constant interchange of dear old Château Latour.
Laura That did impress Edward. I could tell.
Tom Hope so.

They hear more laughter

Laura (*smiling*) What's happening, do you think?
Tom Edward's enchanting Mary Dickinson.
Laura He's always liked women. But I trust him.
Tom Quite right too. (*He takes his hand from her knee*)
Laura He never goes further than mild flirting.
Tom Probably not. Once you're older, time's never on the side of infidelity ... there's no time for all the palaver involved. You have to be a tougher man than me to enjoy hiring a hotel room for an afternoon, the obligatory conversation before you can decently get on with the undressing ... though

decently is hardly the word ... You get sick of all that in middle age. Flirting's all there's time for. So wives of really busy men should feel quite secure.

Laura Oh I do.

Tom You could have relied on me, had we married. I can't be bothered even to flirt.

Laura (*after a pause. blushing*) Had we married? Did you ever think of that?

Tom *No* — I mean, I don't think so, Laura. Did you?

Laura (*shaking her head*) It would never have worked. I'm much too ordinary.

Tom (*polite*) Wouldn't say that ... (*He looks down at her feet*) You still have extraordinarily beautiful feet. I remember that whenever we walked down a street, you insisted we stop and look in all the shoeshop windows.

Laura Lots of women do that.

Tom For your feet, it was a pleasure to buy shoes.

Laura You never bought me a single pair ——

Tom Didn't I? Memory's on the blink again. Hair greying, back aching, teeth loosening. Everything's sliding.

Laura (*smiling*) I couldn't tell. You're exactly the same, to me.

Tom I'm not, you know. (*Pause, thinking*) I could have sworn I bought you a pair of bright blue ——

Laura It must have been someone else.

Tom Anyway, it's very good to see you again. (*Pause*) Laura Dora.

Edward and Alice enter. Edward, glass in hand, has his arm about her, Alice is carrying the ashtrays

Edward (*to Tom*) I found your wife dealing with practicalities.

Some slight confusion as Tom collects the bottle of wine and Alice puts back the ashtrays

Tom Where's Mrs ... Mary?

Edward I left her blowing out the candles. Suppose she's gone upstairs.

Alice She's already been upstairs.

Tom Bet you she's slipped out to the terrace, wants to see it by moonlight. (*He poises the bottle over Edward's glass*)

Alice (*quietly*) Bet you she doesn't.

Laura (*shrieking too loudly*) Edward!

They are all startled

Edward (*snapping*) You can drive. (*He allows Tom to pour half a glass*)

Tom (*to Alice*) Know what I thought? I thought they might like a little preview of the floodlighting. Give them some idea of what it'll be like next year.

Alice raises questioning eyebrows to Edward and Laura

Laura Lovely!

Tom Only I shall need someone to help me shift the lights. (*He goes towards the terrace*)

Edward (*reluctant*) Let me.

Laura (*to Tom*) No, no. I'll come. (*She gets up*)

Tom Laura will manage. Come on. (*To Edward*) You have a nice talk to my wife.

Both smile

(*To Laura*) Memory lane ...

Tom and Laura exit

From opposite sides of the room, Edward and Alice look at each other. Alice eventually breaks off the gaze, goes and sits down. Edward moves near her, looks down upon her. Long silence

Edward Well, at least we've got his permission. It's all going fine.

Alice So far.

Edward (*looking at his watch*) Not long and it'll be over for another twenty years. (*He sits*) Do you know what I found most difficult at dinner? Remembering not to speak our language.

Alice What language?

Edward Well, you know. The general shorthand we once used.

Alice I don't remember that.

Edward I don't believe you. (*Pause*) Teasle.

Alice (*wincing*) Edward, please. I'm sorry if it was so hard for you. In fact, your attention seemed to be almost wholly on Mary Dickinson.

Edward Nonsense! And our legs beneath the table, almost touching. It was quite hard not to remember — well, this and that. Marvellous times.

Alice Really? I had no such problems.

Edward You impervious old thing! I looked at you staring into the distance, wondering if we were thinking the same thing.

Alice I was thinking about sin. What can she be doing up there?

Edward *Sin!* So was I. Coincidence strikes again, after all these years. We often used to think alike. (*Quietly*) You know, I can't imagine why I ever let you go.

Alice (*cajoling*) Edward! There was never any question of staying together! We had a very merry affair but we never deluded ourselves that it was anything more than that ... Quite rightly, you took the precaution of not proposing.

Edward I remember loving you passionately.

Alice Rubbish!

Edward I remember ... going out of my way to do all sorts of things for you I would never have done for anyone else.

Alice (*amused*) Like what?

Edward Well. (*Pause*) Precise detail escapes me. Didn't I once give you a crocodile bag?

Alice You tried. Said it was one your mother never used. I didn't take it.

Edward Must have given it to someone else.

Alice In matters of the heart, memory adds a kind of general benevolence to events — a kindly illusion we like to believe in years later, though secretly know it wasn't quite the truth.

Edward You could be right — but don't you remember — don't you remember anything about us at all?

Alice Of course I do! You were my most rural episode. I'll never forget all that walking!

Edward And are there no feelings left? I mean, now?

Alice (*shaking her head*) Sorry to disappoint, but nothing more than the ordinary warmth that comes from something shared in the past. But then I can't think why you expected ——

Edward Oh I didn't expect, exactly. Just a faint hope, I suppose ...

Alice It was so long ago. And on the Richter scale of love affairs not, well — graph shaking, was it?

Edward True, true. All the same, my heart missed a funny beat yesterday when I saw you on that chair. So I thought that possibly, meeting tonight, yours might ... miss a few beats too.

Alice (*nicely*) Quite steady, I'm afraid.

Edward So no good asking you out to lunch for old time's sake?

Alice Best way to preserve old times is to leave them well alone.

Edward (*mock sad*) I can see nostalgia's getting me nowhere. I give up! All hopes dashed. Case of dead embers, what?

Alice At least there's something wonderfully safe about old flames that have no hope of re-igniting. Safe as good marriage itself. Scarcely a day goes by, you know, when I don't give thanks for being married to Tom.

Edward Have to say we're pretty lucky too, Laura and me. The art, I suppose, is in both parties pulling their weight. Then you can be quite sure nothing will rock the boat.

Tom enters with Laura who stays on the terrace just outside the open french windows

Tom Everything ready to go.
Laura It's such a good idea.
Tom Take your seats.
Laura Edward, you won't see from there.
Alice Shall I fetch Mary Dickinson?
Tom Let's have some music.
Alice Oh, Tom.
Tom Can't have *lumière* without any *son*.
Laura It's wonderfully warm out here, Edward.
Edward I'll be fine here.
Tom Now are we all ready? Here goes.

Tom switches off the lights in the room and turns on the garden lights. We see a faint glow of lumière outside

Laura It's lovely, Tom!
Tom Glad you like it. Of course, it's got some way to go. And obviously you can't get the full effect from here. But next summer, sitting on the terrace, we'll be able to look down on the whole lighted garden — right down to the silver birches. We need some booster lights at the bottom.
Laura Lovely!
Tom There's quite an art in floodlighting. I'm learning slowly. (*He turns on the music*)

Mary enters. Dazed by darkness, she stumbles towards Tom, holding her empty glass. By now she is plainly affected by more drink

Mary What on earth are you all doing in the dark?
Alice Admiring Tom's floodlights.
Tom (*taking a few steps to distance himself from Mary, shouting*) When Alice and I were first married, we went to one of those *son et lumière* things at Versailles. It was quite a new tourist attraction, then.
Alice Fontainebleau, actually.

Alice exits to the kitchen

Lit only by floodlighting outside, all action is difficult to see. Behind Laura and Edward's back Mary moves nearer to Tom, ending up dangerously close to him. The exchange between Laura and Edward shows they are innocent of what's going on. Mary holds out her empty glass to Tom. He shakes his head emphatically

Laura (*shouting above the music to Edward*) Shouldn't we have something like this at home?

Edward Pretentious in a garden our size.

Mary puts down her glass

Laura Just a single bulb under the japonica.

Edward No! Absolutely no!

Laura You're always so ... (*She snatches his glass from him*) For heaven's sake. I'm going to get you some coffee.

Laura exits fast in the poor light

Edward stands. He's not comically drunk but we can see all the wine has had an effect

Edward (*peering towards Tom and Mary*) Oh, so you're back? Jolly impressive show, Tom. (*He looks vaguely about for Laura*) Can't imagine why Laura's always fussing about breathalysing, coffee ...

Edward exits

Mary (*putting a quick hand on Tom's arm; softly accelerating all her power to attract him*) Hallo, Tom.

Tom (*alarmed, but playing for lightness*) Thank you, Mig. (*He looks at his watch*) I'd say we've done pretty well, so far.

Mary (*laughing, raising her glass to Tom*) I'm not drunk, darling. I've had just enough to give me courage to change my mind. (*She puts a hand on Tom's arm*) No more good behaviour!

Tom removes her hand

Tom (*nicely*) You promised you wouldn't cause a scene.

Mary Promises! Huh! Not to be relied on when circumstances change — remember? Circumstances have changed, for me, this very evening. I came expecting to find absolute solidarity between my old lover and his wife. But you're not as secure as you like to make out, are you? That means there's still — a measure of hope for me. Besides, you can't pretend. I know when you want me. (*She flings herself on Tom, trying to clamp her mouth to his*) Kiss me!

Tom, enraged, pushes her quite hard but not viciously. She falls

Tom Get up!

Mary Tom! (*Quickly sitting up, rubbing her shoulder, she looks up smiling, seductive*) You've certainly changed. I rather like it like this ... so fierce.

Laura enters with a pot of coffee

Laura Whatever's happened?

Tom She stumbled. (*He switches off the music*)

Laura Let's put some lights on.

Laura barges about looking for switches

Edward comes in carrying yet another bottle of wine

He sees Mary still rubbing her shoulder with exaggerated anxiety

Edward I say ... what's happened?

Tom She fell.

Laura Where are the light switches?

Tom I'll do it, Laura. (*He switches on the lights*)

Edward That's better. Our revels are all ended, now, Tom, what? (*To Mary*) You all right? (*He gives Mary a hand up*)

Mary Fine, fine.

Edward (*to Tom*) Marvellous show and all that. Real sense of *son* ... (*He helps Mary to a chair*) Might a restoring brandy be the order of the day? If Tom's cognac is half as good as his Latour — which I don't doubt ... May I, Tom?

Mary Tom's the perfect host!

Alice enters

Tom Oh, there you are Alice. Show's over.

Laura (*to Mary*) Are you really all right?

Mary (*irritated*) Yes, thank you.

Laura (*to Alice*) Mary tripped in the dark.

Edward We shouldn't have risked such authentic darkness, if you ask me. Lack of *lumière* is something of a hazard.

Laura hands him a mug of coffee

Tom Of course we should have! How can you expect any effect from floodlighting unless you're sitting in bloody darkness?

He stomps over to the french windows, pulling a torch from his pocket. He exits

Laura (*looking from Mary to Edward*) Oh dear. I thought it was terribly pretty. Next year, Edward ...

Edward Do stop going on, Laura. If you think I'm going to spend precious time turning our pocket handkerchief backyard into some kind of joke Versailles ... you've another ——

Laura (*conspiratorially, to Mary*) I may persuade him in the end!

Tom comes in through the french windows — his crashing entrance suggests he may have it in mind to deflect whatever is Mary's plan

Tom There's another one!

Alice Not another one?

Tom Yes, just by the terrace! It wasn't there before dinner.

Laura Another what?

Tom Molehill.

Edward (*to break a silence*) Ah.

Tom and Alice exchange a slight smile

Tom Sorry. "Barrister almost breaks up party", one thing and another ...

Laura (*small shriek*) Tom! You still speak in headlines. (*To Alice*) You know, I always used to say Tom should be a journalist ——

Alice Did you?

Laura I always thought he had a natural flair for ——

Tom (*to Edward, cutting off Laura with a wave of his hand*) Terrible trouble with moles this year, we're having. Lawn's ruined, but I can't quite bring myself to exterminate them in any of the ghastly ways recommended.

Laura We don't have moles in London, luckily.

Tom Suppose not. Moles can't like London. Understandable.

Edward (*quietly*) We did have one, once.

Laura Did we? I don't remember.

Edward Got rid of the little bugger in a trice.

Tom How?

Edward Wouldn't like to tell you.

Laura (*to Edward, petulant*) You never told me.

Tom (*to Edward*) I'd like to know.

Edward Don't press me!

Tom I'm not that squeamish.

Edward (*after a long pause; looking about, seeing something is up*) No.

Tom and Edward regard each other with a certain good-humoured combativeness

Tom I suppose it was horrible?
Edward That's right.

Mary gets up. Tom glances at her at last, uneasy. He speaks while watching her make her way to the french windows. All eyes follow Mary's progress

Tom (*on automatic pilot*) Funny thing I learned about moles the other day. Their storage system. Do you know how moles store their worms?

Silence. No-one is really concentrating on Tom

They don't bite them in half and kill them, as you might suppose. They tie them in knots. Imagine that!

Laura drags her look from Mary, who is now standing with her back to everyone looking out on to the terrace

Laura (*to Tom*) How amazing!

Mary spins round, arms folded under her breasts. Her scornful eyes pass over them

Mary I don't believe this! (*She laughs*) Butter mountains, terraces, knotted worms ... what an evening!
Laura (*innocently*) What do you mean?
Mary We could have spent our time in much more interesting conversation. Concerning the truth. It's a rather peculiar evening, isn't it? Four old lovers, reunited? I would have thought your mutual metamorphosis a fascinating subject. The change from the unfettered lovers you once were to the set-in-concrete married couple you've become ——
Edward I think we're a bit beyond such silly truth games, Mary. I don't think we came for anything like that.
Mary Dear sweet innocent Edward! Have you found what you came for? Have you all discovered how you feel, now, years after the fires burned out? Alice? Laura? Any small flames, perhaps, stirring among the ashes? Tom?
Edward (*indignantly*) I don't know what you're trying to say, but whatever it is I don't think you'd better go on ——
Laura *Edward!*
Edward Be quiet, Laura.
Laura Do sit down.
Mary It's the hypocrisy I mind about.
Edward Hypocrisy?

Mary Yes, Edward. The belief that if everyone's polite enough it doesn't matter how deep the suffering beneath the façade. But when concealed anguish eventually erupts, there's no knowing what might happen.

Edward None of us has the faintest idea what you're ... rambling on about — it's not the sort of dinner party behaviour one would expect.

Mary Not half an hour ago, alone in the dining-room, you were telling me I had a beautiful mouth, beautiful breasts and taking down my telephone number!

Laura *Edward!*

Edward (*to Laura*) She exaggerates.

Mary (*to Edward*) At least I'm more honest than you. (*Nodding towards Tom*) More honest than him.

Laura (*to Edward*) Did you really take her telephone number?

Mary (*smiling*) He did.

Laura Edward! What do you mean by this? You're not the sort of man who goes round indiscriminately collecting women's telephone numbers!

Mary laughs

You've never been that sort of husband, thank goodness. I mean, I know you've always had an eye for a pretty woman. But I thought it was only an eye ...

Mary Such faith!

Edward (*to Laura, sitting beside her on the sofa*) Of course it's only an eye, silly. Dammit, we often laugh about it, don't we? Joke.

Mary Perhaps it's not a joke.

Edward We come back from a party, you say "Bet you fancied that girl in the blue dress". I say, "Right" as usual. Given half a chance! Course it's a joke.

Laura suddenly plunges her hand into one of Edward's pockets

What are you doing? Hey, stop it!

Laura Where is it?

Edward Where's what? (*Annoyed*) Get off me.

In the scuffle Laura succeeds in pulling a small piece of torn paper from Edward's pocket. She holds it up, triumphant

Laura There! Here it is! What were you going to do with it, tell me that?

Edward (*flustered*) Do with it? What does one do with telephone numbers? One either loses them or rings them.

Laura (*incredulous*) You would have rung her, asked her out, paid some huge restaurant bill even though you've been objecting to my getting a new washing machine — *seduced* her!

Edward Jealousy the great exaggerator — come off it, Laura. You know you're being ridiculous. She'd have been lucky to get so much as a drink out of me ——

Laura I don't believe you. (*She tears up the paper*)

Mary Calm yourself Laura. I doubt your husband would have rung me. He's a timid man.

Laura (*affronted*) Edward is not a timid man! (*Beat*) Would that he were.

Mary This is all rather beside the point: To be honest, it's good to be here at least. See it all for myself.

Alice What?

Mary Nice bedroom Alice, I liked it.

Alice What do you mean?

Mary I liked the fact that among the ornaments on your shelf was a small ebony pebble, one of the kind I used to find on the beach at home and gave to the friends I loved.

Mary looks at Tom. Alice also looks at Tom. The awful realization is hardening. Then, dignified, Alice turns her back to Mary

Alice I don't know what she means, Tom.

Mary I liked your bed, too.

Alice (*spinning back round to face her*) Our *bed*?

Mary I took the liberty of lying on it for a moment. Imagining. A nice little symbolic gesture, I thought.

Alice (*quietly*) You lay on our bed?

Laura Edward won't even let the cat on our bed!

Mary (*ignoring her*) Oh, I dare do anything now. I'm free. Free to exercise my rights as the woman who suddenly became inconvenient. You'll find the dent left by my body on top of the older, deeper dent left by yours ——

Edward This is ... intolerable ...

Laura (*turning to Edward*) One minute you want her telephone number — the next you're condemning her for having taken a short rest!

Edward Keep your irrelevancies out of this, Laura. Mrs Dickinson, I think you'd better go. Now. Out, out.

Mary Damn spot! Don't worry, I'll go when I've said my bit ——

Laura Irrelevancies! You call propositioning an unbeknown woman at dinner an irrelevance? How many years has this been going on?

Edward (*turning on Laura, icily*) If you'd spent less time being the perfect wife, all that stifling compliance, demeaning willingness to please, I'd have had less need to remind myself what unreasonable, difficult, exciting women are like!

Laura (*sadly wailing*) Dear Jesus! Is there nothing a wife can do right? (*She turns away to stifle a sob*)

Edward I only said *remind* myself. Reminding isn't fornicating, for heaven's sake. (*To Mary, angrily*) You started all this. You tricked us into bringing you here. What for?

Mary (*calmly*) Ask Tom. Tom knows why I've come. Tom knows what I have to say.

Alice (*to Tom, finally realizing*) Tom?

Mary Tom knows why I'm here. He tried to make me go. But I refused, didn't I Tom?

Tom You promised ——

Mary Yes, yes. I promised to behave and now I'm breaking that promise. Just as you broke promises to me. Promises among adulterers, it seems, are worthless.

Laura (*sniffing, making a rather pathetic attempt to be firm and calm*) Mrs Dickinson, I think we should take you home now before we get in to something we'll all regret.

Mary (*smiling to Laura*) Don't worry, Laura. I'll go quietly. I'm not mad. I haven't come here bent on revenge, destruction. I've come here simply to see, to have my say at last, and to go again.

Tom For God's sake, Mary ...

Mary (*beginning quietly*) You ...

Tom Please.

Mary ignores him, her eyes sweep round the room and rest on Alice

Mary You! But for you, we would have had the rest of our lives together, Tom and me — you realize that? But no! I lost out to the marriage! He couldn't face the disruption of ending it. Given the choice, he opted for the institution rather than the passion. Until that moment, I would not have accused him of cowardice.

Edward (*quietly*) I don't think any of us wants to hear this sort of stuff, Mrs Dickinson ——

Mary (*to Edward*) You were willing enough to listen to what I had to say after dinner. You swallowed my flattery easily enough ——

Laura (*to Mary*) Flattery? (*To Edward*) What flattery?

Edward She merely praised my status in the wine trade ...

Laura I can't believe you any more.

Edward You misinterpret everything, Laura ... I propose we chuck Mrs Dickinson out if she shows any more signs of overstaying her welcome. With force, if necessary. (*He bangs himself on the chest*)

Laura Who'd believe so innocent an evening. Dear God, what's happening?

Mary You're being forced to look at yourselves as you really are. Four smug, happily married people. Laura of the once wild nail polish bravely hiding her daily fears about Edward, known to pounce as soon as his wife's back is turned. Then, Alice, here, her life so empty she has to ape the student and glut her boredom in books. As for Tom ... Tom still secretly battling against his love for me and not succeeding for a single moment. But miraculously, you're all still married!

Edward Well of course we are!

Laura (*a hesitant echo*) Of course we are!

Edward Decent married people know how to behave, know the rules ... Marriage ought to be the object of universal respect, someone once said.

Alice (*quietly*) Balzac!

Mary (*snapping, triumphant*) Look at you. The smug married front — a little frayed in the last few minutes but still battling to keep up a good face to the world. I despise it! I despise you all, for your hypocrisy. I gave myself to Tom completely for two years.

Alice Two years?

Mary Though of course you can't know, you faithful wives, what it's like to be the mistress ... willing to be squeezed in between appointments, left in a hurry, hustled out of sight, kept from friends, hidden, always hidden. Discarded in summer, abandoned at Christmas. Wanting all, I had to accept that no man wants the whole of a mistress — just those parts convenient to him.

Edward Isn't that the whole point of a mistress?

Laura (*shocked*) Edward! That's going too far! Surely a mistress has every right ——

Edward (*smiling sarcastically*) Are you now siding with Mrs Dickinson?

Laura Oh goodness, this is terrible. If I was a mistress ——

Edward You ... are not ... mistress material.

Mary It wasn't marriage to Tom I was after. In my opinion the odds on a happy marriage are so extraordinarily low it's a wonder the majority of the population keep taking the risk. After all, the appeal of romance is lethal, except in the short term. The thing that attracts men and women together rarely binds them. So, logically, there's little hope.

Laura I think I could have been a mistress if I'd tried.

Mary (*laughing*) What an ambition.

Laura (*dignified and calm now she has made her announcement*) It was no ambition of mine. I'd never thought there was any necessity. Perhaps, if I had, Edward would have found me more exciting.

Edward (*faintly ashamed*) Don't be silly, Laura. What's got into you? No need for all this dirty linen ——

Laura (*turning on Mary*) As for your dislike of hypocrisy, where does your husband come into all this?

Mary There's no hypocrisy between us. Gerald wanted to marry the small part of me that was left over after loving Tom. We're content in our understanding, we don't pretend it's any more than that.

Edward Oh my God!

Mary I want you to know that I could never give up the intense desire to see what it was Tom couldn't leave. Tom was so discreet, you see. He would never describe any of his private — well, official life. He hardly ever talked about you, except to say that you were his wife and he couldn't leave his wife. (*Pause, catch of breath*) Now I've seen and I don't understand. Because I know he still loves me. I looked at him tonight and I know he still loves me. If you ask him now if it is the truth, he could not lie to you. He loves me.

Alice (*moving close to Tom, taking his arm*) Tom? Is that the truth?

Tom (*bluff*) Such discussions must be private between barrister and wife — please, Alice.

Mary There! He doesn't deny it!

Alice I imagine your mission is complete Mrs Dickinson. You've had your say. You've seen what you wanted to see, our house, our kitchen, our bed. You've made your mark. You've scrutinized me, the wife. And I think you should be on your way now.

Mary Your husband is a torn man, Alice! Torn between what he actually desires and what duty demands of him.

Alice Torn? Wives are often stumbling blocks I know. Shall I tell you my side of the story? How it was in this house?

Tom We've had enough confessions, Alice.

Alice I insist. It's only fair. I first thought there was something up when Tom became a little ... sharper, you could call it. More alert. After so many years of marriage you don't need words to understand there's a quickening in your husband's blood. I was sometimes tempted by the thought of competing, trying in areas I so often fail. I made some effort never to run out of coffee, never to throw away *The Times* before he'd read it. But then — no, I thought. He's getting enough sparkle with whoever it is. He'd want things to be normal at home. So I watched. I waited. Trusting he would work it out, determined not to add to his problems by questions.

Edward (*to Laura*) There's good behaviour for you!

Alice (*to Mary*) You may think such reticence is very peculiar. But one of the useful things about a good marriage is that over the years you work out a behaviour pattern that suits you both, and stick to it. We went on, normally to outward appearances. As close as ever, in our funny way.

Mary (*to Tom*) While all the time *we* were as close as ever. Your barrister's skill at double dealing must have been strained to the hilt.

Edward (*jumping up*) If I may interrupt for a moment here, I'd like to put forward the motion, before things get any more out of hand ——

Laura This isn't a board meeting! Do be quiet, Edward. You've said too much already. You've ——

Alice (*turning back to Mary*) One morning Tom said it was time for a new greenhouse, ready for his retirement — I knew the worst was over then. He was much happier. He came home, a rainy evening, his old self. "Thank you for waiting," he said. "I knew you would." All's over. "Barrister's back on course"! No explanation needed.

Mary (*incredulous laugh*) You believed him?

Alice Of course I believed him. The past, to Tom, is dead. Perhaps you didn't know that. Nothing can revive it, can it Tom? Not even an ill-considered and over-dramatic appearance like this. So you better not do any hoping ... for Tom's an honourable man ——

Mary Nothing can ever stop my hope, my love for Tom ——

Alice But surely you're not hoping to break all this up? Take Tom away?

Mary When you love someone completely you're driven to trying to solve impossible equations such as Tom, Alice, me. I've dallied with the idea that Tom might like a time-share arrangement.

Tom shakes his head

So many men imagine an outside interest, to relieve the pressures of monogamy, will make them better husbands. But I don't think Alice would want that any more than me. So, it's Tom's choice. He can either give up his wife, before it's too late, and take this last chance of me. Or he can stay — to what? Now Alice knows the truth. If he has the guts, he'll leave ...

Alice (*to Mary, quietly*) Never! Tom would never leave me for you. Because he knows where his priorities lie ... his wife comes first. His trust is in his marriage. The institution you referred to with such scorn is not an easy one. It needs years of false starts and new attempts before the right way can be agreed. Marriage may be of no consequence to you. But those of us who've gone into it with firmness of purpose have reason to believe it's the soundest structure one can opt for in this unsound life. Those of us, in other words, who *like* our marriages, can't easily be persuaded to let them go. So when it comes to the weighing up, Mrs Dickinson, unless it's been something much more serious than your little ... interlude with Tom — it's marriage that wins.

Mary (*beginning to crack*) A "little interlude" was it?

Tom puts a hand on Alice's shoulder. Mary looks at them scornfully

We'll see about that, won't we Tom?

Tom I think you should go now.

Brief silence. Mary doesn't move

Mig.

Mary Very well. I'll leave you to the safety of your marriages. (*She goes towards the terrace*)

Alice You can't get out that way.

Mary Funny: you spend years wondering how to get in to a house and then, when you manage it at last, you find you can't get out. Can I get a taxi in the village?

Alice You might be able to catch the last train.

Mary Thank you. (*She goes to the door and pauses*) However much Tom loves you, his wife, Alice, he's equally bound to me. Exclusive love? Huh! There's no such thing.

Mary exits

A moment's silence. Edward puts out a hand to Laura

Edward Well, I suppose we'd better drop her off at the station. It's time we were on our way too, darling.

Laura Don't you "darling" me! She was right about hypocrisy. (*She looks hard at his dishevelment*) I'll drive, or we'll end this memorable evening in a ditch.

Edward (*placatory*) Come on. Alice, hope you don't mind if Laura and I shoot off, do you? I don't think there's much we can —— (*He extends his hand to Laura*)

Laura (*getting up, pointedly refusing Edward's hand*) If there's any way we can help?

Alice No.

Laura (*automatically*) Well then, thank you both so much for a ——

Edward Come on, Laura.

He firmly takes her arm but as they go she struggles free

Bye!

Edward and Laura exit

Long shocked silence

Tom Well, here we are. Where does it leave us, Alice?

Alice shakes her head. Pause

Alice Did she give you the pebble?

Tom nods. Alice sighs

I imagine she's ... deteriorated.

Tom I suppose all that rage, festering over the years.

Alice (*suddenly fierce*) You can't be "equally bound" to her!

Tom Of course not.

Alice At least she's gone. What will she do now?

Tom In her present mood ...

Alice She's not just going to go away, is she?

Tom Probably not.

Alice You heard what she said. She feels free now to have her revenge. Her dent in the bed was just a beginning. I know what'll follow. She'll haunt us, taunt us. Spring up in our path, confront, make scenes. There are women like that.

Tom, playing for time, picks up Alice's glasses, fiddles with them. They snap in his shaky hand

Tom Look what I've gone and done. I'm so sorry.

Alice (*almost cracking, giving a great wail*) Oh no! How'll I manage tomorrow?

Tom Don't worry. I'll ... (*He searches in a drawer for a plaster*)

Pause

Alice How could you have loved such a woman?

Tom (*mending her glasses*) I've often wondered. I've often wondered — was it love? Was it vanity? Or was it just the nefarious excitement of the conquest that sometimes overcomes the stablest of men? The thing about marriage, it's a perpetual crisis of alternatives. Whether to tell the truth or to deceive, to protect or to hurt, to speak one's mind or keep one's silence. A dozen such decisions are sent to try us each day, aren't they? Battling with them is all part of the ritual. (*He brings back Alice's mended glasses*)

Alice Thanks.

Tom But then — very rarely, thank God — comes a more crucial decision: whether to be tempted or to resist, whether to allow oneself to be bewitched, risking all the consequences, or to say, no! Go! This is not for me. (*He meets Alice's eye*) I love my wife.

Alive She was wrong about the smugness.

Tom nods

Nothing smug about a thriving marriage. Too much to do keeping from the knife's edge. Tom, it's very late.

Tom I'd better go. Least I can do is to leave without a fuss.

Alice Go? Where to? To her?

Tom Could postpone departure till the morning, I suppose. Bit late now for "Barrister to find a bed". We could work things out, no need to be unfriendly. Half my worldly goods are yours, of course. The terrace, I'm only sorry it's not finished for you.

Alice (*struggling to conceal alarm*) How would I ...?

Tom I could leave instructions about the planting.

Pause. He watches her remove her earrings

What are you doing?

Alice Thinking.

Tom Those are yours. I wouldn't want them back. I remember that day, "Barrister felt need to give wife diamonds". I'm trying to make this ending easy, civilized.

Alice Ending?

Tom You said if she came into our lives again that would be the end.

Alice (*putting the earrings in her pocket*) You'd have to tell me very specifically where things should go. The lavender — where did you say you wanted the lavender?

Tom (*faint smile*) I'd draw you a detailed plan. Surely you don't believe I ever felt ——

Alice I don't know what you felt. Was it love?

Tom Love! The line between love and infatuation is eternally confusing, even to old hands. Infatuation is a baser thing, I suppose. To call it love is to dignify its extremes, to justify it, to hope for more understanding ——

Alice (*impatient*) Tom! It's too late for such cheap philosophies. Did you love her?

Tom I don't know.

Alice And what do you feel now? What do you want?

Tom (*struggling with himself*) I want you, our marriage. I feel the most profound desire never to see or hear from Mrs Dickinson again.

Alice How can I believe you? I know too much ——

Tom I'm sorry.

The telephone rings

Alice Edward and Laura, to apologize? (*She goes to answer it*)

Tom brushes past her, snatches up the receiver. He listens for a moment, then puts it down

Tom The campaign's begun.

Alice What did I tell you?

Tom You said all those things so passionately in favour of marriage. (*He goes to her and touches each cheek lightly with a finger*)
Alice I meant them.

The telephone rings again. Alice covers it with a cushion

Tom See, she's losing already!
Alice We've all lost. (*Pause*) I'm going to bed. Please bolt the doors.

Tom goes to the french windows, shuts the bolts, and remains looking out, his back to Alice

Tom Terrace so damn near finished ... think you can manage?
Alice Not without you — no.
Tom Then might "Barrister put in a bid to see the whole thing through"?

Alice shrugs but with another faint smile. The telephone rings for the third time. With sudden spirit, Alice snatches up a small rug from the floor and throws it over the cushions

Alice Why don't you unplug the bloody thing?
Tom Why don't you?

The ringing stops

    She won't ring again.

Alice looks sceptical

    I know her.
Alice Knew her.

They observe each other in a moment's silence

Tom She'll wake up in the morning — sober, shaken, satisfied she's made her scene. She'll see the pointlessness of going on.

Alice opens the door. We see she is exhausted but wants to believe him

Alice Perhaps. Sleep well. We need the morning.
Tom Good-night.

    Alice exits

Tom stands looking after her for a moment. His eyes move to the silent telephone, he begins to uncover it, throwing the rug and cushions down with confident abandon. Then he goes to the sofa, sits, dazed. The telephone begins to ring again. Tom covers his head with his hands

Fade to Black-out

CURTAIN

FURNITURE AND PROPERTY LIST

ACT I
SCENE 1

On stage: Large table. *On it*: pencil, papers, letter, gardeners' catalogues, teapot,
5 mugs, plate with half-eaten sandwich, 2 seed trays planted with
small green shoots, radio, ashtray
4 wooden chairs. *On one*: large man's jersey
Sofa. *On it*: cushions with pair of gold-rimmed glasses down side of
one. *On arm*: pile of books
Old dresser. *On shelves*: mugs, jars, glasses. *In drawer*: plaster. *On top*:
tray of drinks with corkscrew, ashtray
Telephone
Pictures on walls
Bookshelves. *On them*: books
Small rug

Off stage: Umbrella (**Alice**)

Personal: **Tom**: watch (worn throughout)

SCENE 2

Set: 2 dinner plates with remains of a meal
2 bottles of partially drunk wine
Large unlit candle on table

Off stage: Tray (**Tom**)

Personal: **Tom**: box of matches

SCENE 3

Reset: 2 boxes of seed trays under table
Tidy up catalogues, papers, books, gold-rimmed glasses, etc. on table

Set: 3 bottles of supermarket wine for **Tom**
Tom's jacket with crumpled tie in pocket

Off stage:	Bottle of Latour wine (**Edward**)
	2 dusty bottles of Latour wine (**Tom**)
	Bunch of parsley (**Alice**)

Personal:	**Tom**: handkerchief
	Mary: pendant on thin gold chain
	Edward: watch (worn throughout)

ACT II

Strike:	Bottles of wine

Set:	Cigarette ends in ashtrays

Off stage:	Bottle of wine (**Alice**)
	Glass with some wine (**Laura**)
	Empty glass (**Mary**)
	Glass (**Edward**)
	Pot of coffee (**Laura**)
	Bottle of wine (**Edward**)

Personal:	**Tom**: practical torch in pocket
	Edward: small piece of torn paper in pocket

LIGHTING PLOT

Practical fittings required: lamps
Interior. The same scene throughout

ACT I, Scene 1. Late afternoon

To open: General interior lighting with daylight effect through french
windows

Cue 1	**Alice**'s and **Tom**'s fingers just touch	(Page 11)
	Fade to black-out	

ACT I, Scene 2. Evening

To open: General interior lighting with practicals on and dusk effect
through french windows

Cue 2	**Tom** and **Alice** move to the door	(Page 16)
	Fade to black-out	

ACT I, Scene 3. Evening

To open: General interior lighting with practicals on and dusk effect
through french windows, fading as the scene progresses

Cue 3	**Alice** " ... quite an asset after all."	(Page 32)
	Fade to black-out	

ACT II

To open: Dim interior lighting with night effect through french windows

Cue 4	**Alice** goes about turning on lights	(Page 33)
	Snap on practicals and covering spots in sequence	
Cue 5	**Tom** switches off room lights	(Page 42)
	Snap off practicals and covering spots in sequence	
Cue 6	**Tom** switches on garden lights	(Page 42)
	Bring up garden lighting	

Cue 7   **Tom** switches on room lights   (Page 44)
            Snap on practicals and covering spots in sequence

Cue 8   **Tom** covers his head with his hands   (Page 57)
            Fade to black-out

EFFECTS PLOT

ACT I

Cue 1	To open *Music*	(Page 1)
Cue 2	**Tom** switches off the record player *Cut music*	(Page 1)
Cue 3	**Tom:** "The dining-room it shall be." *Telephone*	(Page 12)
Cue 4	**Tom:** "Not like you." *Doorbell*	(Page 17)
Cue 5	**Alice:** " ... he waved at *me* ..." *Doorbell*	(Page 17)
Cue 6	**Tom, Edward** and **Alice** exit. Pause *Doorbell*	(Page 23)

ACT II

Cue 7	**Tom** turns on the music *Music*	(Page 42)
Cue 8	**Tom:** "She stumbled." (He switches off the music) *Cut music*	(Page 44)
Cue 9	**Tom:** "I'm sorry." *Telephone*	(Page 55)
Cue 10	**Alice:** "I meant them." *Telephone*	(Page 56)
Cue 11	**Alice** shrugs *Telephone; continue*	(Page 56)
Cue 12	**Tom:** "Why don't you?" *Telephone stops*	(Page 56)
Cue 13	**Tom** sits, dazed *Telephone*	(Page 57)